JLPT-N5 CHARACTERS

LANGUAGE WORKBOOK FOR BEGINNERS

- ☑ Master your first Kanji, Step-by-Step
- ☑ Understand Kanji Meanings and Stroke Order
- ☑ Stroke Order Diagrams and Writing Tips

© Copyright 2022 George Tanaka - All Rights Reserved

POLYSCHOLAR

www.polyscholar.com

© Copyright 2022 George Tanaka - All Rights Reserved

Legal Notice: This book is copyright protected. This book is only for personal use. The content contained within this book may not be reproduced, duplicated or transmitted without direct written permission from the author or the publisher. You cannot amend, distribute, sell, use, quote or paraphrase any part of the content within this book, without the consent of the author or publisher.

# CONTENTS

| 1 | Kanji | 4 |
| 2 | Hiragana & Katakana Charta | 15 |
| 3 | Kanji N5 Stroke Order Practice | 25 |
| 4 | Genkouyoushi | 106 |
| 5 | Flash Cards | 122 |
| 7 | Thank You | 137 |

Tip: *This book works best with gel pens, pencils, biros and similar media. Take care with markers and ink, as heavy or wet media may result in paper bleed or transfer through to the pages below. Here are some test boxes to check how suitable your pens will be:*

## THE SCIENCE OF KANJI

By now in your Japanese study, you have probably heard about kanji, one of the most daunting parts for new learners starting Japanese. Mastering kanji, like any other part of a language, takes lots of dedication and time, but this book is specially designed to show you how to begin learning kanji with ease!

Japanese kanji (漢字) have been called the third alphabet of the language, but this is a bit of a misnomer. As English speakers learning hiragana and katakana, you have probably noticed the similarities between the English alphabet and these Japanese syllabaries. Both are designed to describe the phonetic sounds of words in their respective languages, but kanji is much different. Imported from the Chinese writing system thousands of years ago, kanji are, like their Chinese relatives, a logographic writing system, which means that each character represents a meaning rather than a specific sound. This means that when reading Japanese, some kanji characters can be read up to 18 different ways! Don't let that scare you off though, as most commonly kanji have only two pronunciations (also known as readings): the kunyomi and the onyomi. The kunyomi reading is used when the character is used to represent a native Japanese word, helpful for differentiating between Japanese's many similar-sounding words. On the other hand, the onyomi reading is used when the characters are being used in the same word as other kanji, usually Chinese loanwords.

# HOW TO USE THIS BOOK

As with learning any language, repetition is one of the fastest ways to soak it up. This workbook contains carefully designed instruction pages that will teach you how to write each character, with space to practice your new-found Japanese calligraphy knowledge:

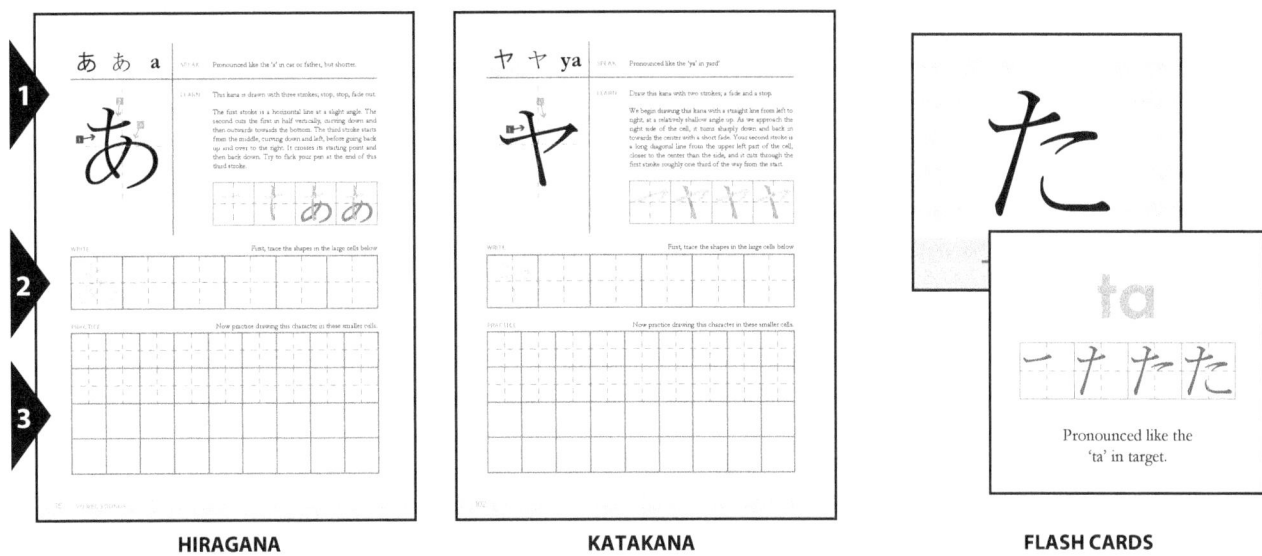

**HIRAGANA**     **KATAKANA**     **FLASH CARDS**

Towards the back of this workbook you will find additional grids that you can use after you learn how to write some *(or even all)* of the Kana - these grid pages are referred to traditionally as *Genkouyoushi (or* 原稿用紙 *in Japanese)* which means 'manuscript paper'.

The final part of this workbook contains a set of flash card style pages that can either be photocopied or cut out. They are a great way to help you memorize the symbols and test your knowledge. *Younger learners should seek help from an adult to cut them out!*

## A BRIEF HISTORY OF JAPANESE AND KANJI

Japanese is one of the many languages in the world that are classified as language isolates, which means that they don't have a known ancestor language or any related languages, other than the Ryukyuan languages spoken in the islands to the south of the mainland. This means that, where English and German are "genetically related" in that they both came from a parent language, called proto-Germanic, and share many of the same words and grammar, Japanese has no known parent or siblings. However, from as early as the 5th century Japan began importing Chinese characters via the Korean peninsula and began to use the Chinese writing system for texts and documents in their own country. This style of writing, called kanbun, was written entirely with Chinese characters, grammar, and syntax, but pronounced with a mix of Chinese and Japanese readings. Sound confusing? It was!

Kanbun has been classified by some scholars as an entirely different creole language, as it would be incomprehensible to the average Chinese or Japanese citizen at the time. Nevertheless, or precisely because of this, it became widely popular with the elite and noble classes, and most of the intellectual and official works from the 9th century until the 20th were written in this style. In fact, the syllabaries hiragana and katakana were developed later, by women in the noble courts who were barred from the rigorous education needed to write in this Chinese-Japanese hybrid. They used a small number of Chinese characters for their sound alone to represent Japanese, and the cursive way of writing these characters became simplified over time into the hiragana we know today. While many in the elite classes preferred writing in this kanbun style, the easy-to-learn hiragana became increasingly popular among non-elites and others who would otherwise be unable to write. Over time the syllabaries and the use of kanji melded together into the Japanese writing we know today, which uses a mixture of all three in everyday writing as well as official texts.

## THERE ARE HOW MANY KANJI?!?!?

After centuries of these characters being imported into Japan, by now there are lots and lots of kanji, by some estimates over 50,000! However, the vast majority of these are non-standard or not in use anymore and won't be encountered outside texts written in Classical Japanese. In fact, the most rigorous kanji aptitude test in Japan for historians and translators only tests about 6,000 characters, with the jōyō kanji (lit. daily-use Chinese characters) being the standard 2,136 characters required to be considered fluent in the language. These jōyō kanji are also what is taught from first grade through the end of high school to Japanese children, so there is plenty of teaching material for these kanji.

## WHERE TO START

But how do these young students start learning all those characters? In much of the same ways, you will be, through repetition, practice, and encountering and using kanji in real-life situations. Many of the first characters you will learn are **pictographic**, meaning they visually represent the meaning associated with them. For instance, the character for tree, 木 (ki), resembles a tree with the central trunk and several branches. The character for river, 川 (kawa), looks like a stream of water rushing down. These pictographic kanji make up only a small amount of the total characters used in modern Japanese but are a good way for students new to logographic languages to get to grips with them. This is also advantageous because many of the first pictographic kanji are put together to make new kanji, so you will come across many new characters and already have a hint at the meaning, or the sound, of the character is.

As characters start to become more complex, many learners use mnemonics to help them remember the meaning of more advanced kanji, which are most often made up of 2 or more parts, called radicals. For instance, a well-known mnemonic for the character 町 (town, machi) is to remember that it is a rice field (田) next to a street (丁), two things that will be found in 100% of Japanese small towns.

As most people learn kanji in a similar order to Japanese grade school students, reading children's books can be a very good way of practicing once you have a solid foundation of characters. Once those ones become easier you can try a more challenging book, or another popular option, manga. As you probably know already, manga are Japanese comic books that in recent years have become extremely popular all over the world. Manga are a great option for people trying to start reading in Japanese because the illustrations help a great deal with understanding the text. If you already can read the characters, then the drawing acts as a good visualization of the words to remember them better. On the other hand, if you can't understand all the words, the words you do understand along with the context of the illustrations makes it much more likely that you will be able to ascertain the meaning of the word or character, all on your own.

## LEARNING TO WRITE KANJI (OR NOT)

So, reading this far, you may be thinking: "Well, if I'm mostly planning to speak and listen in Japanese, I just need to learn hiragana and katakana. I can write everything in the language with those characters and therefore don't need to learn how to write kanji at all."

And to an extent, this is true. You could theoretically become fluent in spoken Japanese without learning a single kanji character and write the next great Japanese novel entirely in hiragana. Everyone who reads it would have a very hard time differentiating between words (Japanese writing doesn't have spaces) and would probably have to sound out most words individually to understand them, as they are so used to reading with kanji. But it is possible. However, if you ever want to be in Japan and understand signs and directions, if you ever want to write anything that is easy to read and understand, if you ever want to read a single sentence in the language, you are going to have to get studying.

## READING (AS A WAY TO LEARN KANJI)

You may hear from some Japanese learning purists that, like the immersion method for learning the spoken component of a language, rather than study programs it is a better use of your time to immerse yourself in written content such as a newspaper and just look up every word you encounter until you start to get it. While this is theoretically possible once you have a basic grasp of grammar and the 2 syllabaries, for the most part, this is destined to simply make you frustrated and make your finger cramp up from looking up so many kanji by hand. As I said above, simply reading is the best way to learn to read Japanese, but only after you have enough of a foundation in the language where you only must look up a couple of words per line. There will be Japanese learners who are exceptions to this and are ready and dedicated enough to repeatedly try to read newspapers day after day, and I'm sure they are going to get great results with enough time, but for most, I recommend waiting for even just a couple months before diving into day-to-day written content for adults.

## WHICH ORDER TO LEARN KANJI

Most kanji classes, apps, and study books will have the characters presented to you in one of 4 main orders, each of them broadly overlapping with each other. The characters in these books will often be ordered according to how kanji are taught to children in Japanese grade schools, from words that make up the building blocks of meaning and conversation (people, sound, hand, home, child, eat, drink, live, etc.) to more abstract and uncommon words as the children get older. Some workbooks will take a more statistical approach and teach characters in order from the most common kanji to the more rare characters. In a similar vein, some are in order from the simplest kanji (一, ichi, meaning 1) to some of the most complicated and dense characters, with stroke numbers (basically, the number of times the pen makes a new stroke when writing the character) in the 20s.

And of course, many study materials, such as this book, base their kanji list on the Japanese Language Proficiency Test, the worldwide standardized measure of a non-native speaker's ability in the language. While the JLPT organization does not release official lists of what characters will or will not be on their tests, after many years of testing instructors have worked out an accurate guideline for what characters are likely to be on any given level of the JLPT, from N5 (basic proficiency) to N1 (native or near-native level proficiency). While all of these ordering methods differ slightly, as stated previously they all for the most part are ordered from the most basic kanji (in meaning and in stroke number) to the more advanced ones.

## WHAT ARE RADICALS?

Radicals are the term for the indivisible building blocks of kanji, the small sets of strokes that are put together differently to make up each character. For instance, the character 魑, meaning "mountain demons", at first glance looks far too complicated to ever write yourself and requires a total of 20 strokes to write, a dauntingly dense kanji even for native speakers. However, if you see it as an arrangement of standardized radicals, a collection of simple smaller components (田, 儿, 厶, 亠, 凵, and 内) put together, it becomes much easier to conceptualize. With some of those same components, we can make the kanji 充 ("enough"), a character with the same constituent parts but a completely different meaning.

## LEARNING KANJI BY RADICALS

As a more advanced method of kanji learning and memorization, some workbooks teach kanji sorted by their **meaning components**, a special class of radical. Meaning components are the component of the kanji that is (usually) on the left-hand side of the character and that gives a hint to the meaning of the kanji. As you learn more kanji you may start to see a pattern, such as that the characters for 汁, 沖, 沈, and 渚 all share those three small dots on the left side of them. That is because those three dots are meant to represent drops of water dripping down, and each of these characters' meanings (broth, open sea, sinking, and shoreline, respectively) have something to do with water or liquidity in a more abstract sense. These radicals, of which there are 214 traditionally, are how characters are sorted in a kanji dictionary and can be very helpful clues as to what the meaning of a character is, especially if you already know the other character of a word it's in.

Some other common radicals used as meaning components you will encounter quickly in your Japanese journey are 月 ("moon"), 火 ("fire"), 木 ("wood"), 金 ("metal"), and 土 ("ground"), all of which are names of the days of the week as well. A few radicals, like 月 (tsuki, moon), mean something completely different when used as a radical inside a kanji. In the case of 月 this is because when it is used as a radical it is a simplified version of 肉 (niku, meat) and indicates the meaning has something to do with flesh. However, once you have these few quirks learned and about 50 meaning radicals figured out, something that will happen a lot sooner than you think, you will have a free hint on a large percentage of the new kanji you encounter, just like that!

## SOUND COMPONENTS

While meaning components are typically on the left side of a kanji, on the right side is what's known as the **sound component**. Most kanji have one radical that hints at the meaning and a sound component that hits at the sound, as well as differentiates the character from others with the same meaning component. Note that the sound component only gives a hint to the Chinese-borrowed reading, the **onyomi**, and not the native Japanese reading of the character (also known as the **kunyomi**), if it has one.

For example, a common sound component to remember is derived from the character 方 (meaning "direction/side", with onyomi reading hou). This character hints at the sound for each of these characters: 肪 (bou), 枋 (hou), 彷 (hou), 訪 (hou), 防 (bou), and many more. As you can see from the ones that are read as bou, this is not a perfect system, but most of the time, if the onyomi isn't the same as the character that the sound component is derived from, it will have at least the consonant or the vowel sound in common.

## SOUND CHANGES IN THE JOURNEY FROM CHINESE TO JAPANESE

As stated, Chinese and Japanese are not genetically related languages (i.e. they did not come from a common ancestor language). However, similar to English and French, the thousands of years of cultural exchange between the two civilizations make many words in both Chinese and Japanese, particularly words describing more complex concepts and processes, sometimes sound quite similar.

For instance, in modern Mandarin Chinese the word for mountain is pronounced shān and written 山. Similarly, in Japanese, 山 is read as "yama" in the native Japanese pronunciation, but read as "san", very similar to the Chinese, when attached to the end of a mountain's name, the same as we say "Mt. ____" in English. So, if we wanted to write "Mount Helena" in Japanese, it would be "ヘレナ山", read as "herena-san". Changes like these are very common in Japanese, and anyone with even a cursory knowledge of Chinese will be coming into their Japanese study with a huge head start, and vice-versa.

## KANJI READINGS: KUN'YOMI AND ON'YOMI

As stated previously, each Japanese kanji character has at least one reading, but most have 2 or more ways they are pronounced when read, one is what is known as a *kun'yomi* reading, and one that is called an *on'yomi* reading. The *kun'yomi* is used when writing native Japanese words using Chinese characters, using the native Japanese pronunciation. On the other hand, the *on'yomi* is the pronunciation that the character originally had in Chinese, with alterations to match Japanese's set of **phonemes** (all the sounds that make up the language). Because of this, the *on'yomi* is most often used when the kanji is put right alongside another *kanji* in the same word, as the whole word was probably originally borrowed from a Chinese word.

In this way, you could think of a kanji as having (usually) one reading, the *on'yomi*, which even means "sound reading", whereas the *kun'yomi*, which roughly means "meaning reading" is meant to represent a native Japanese word as a sort of visual shortcut.

As you can probably imagine, which one of these readings to use when reading out loud is one of the most difficult parts of the language for Japanese learners to grasp, and is largely one of those things that simply takes time to remember the reading for each phrase or context a character is in. However, there are some general rules for when to use one or the other. As mentioned earlier, if two kanji are together in the same word there is a very high probability both characters will be read with their on'yomi. If the kanji is by itself, or next to hiragana, it is probably going to be read with its kun'yomi. As an easy way to remember this, notice that when the kanji is next to characters borrowed from Chinese (i.e. other kanji), it will use the Chinese borrowed reading, but when the kanji is next to native Japanese characters (i.e. hiragana) it will use the native Japanese pronunciation. In addition, Japanese names for people and places will almost always use the kun'yomi. Of course, as with any rule in language, these rules have many exceptions that will sadly take lots of trial and error to memorize. Some words even use the same character but mean different things depending on whether you use the on'yomi or the kun'yomi! But with time it will all start to make sense, and the basic rules I laid out will carry you triumphantly through a large percentage of the words you encounter.

## STROKE ORDER

When writing kanji, every character has one specific method of writing it out that is the "correct" way to write it. This is known as the **stroke order**. Don't get too worried, however, as there are some simple rules to follow that will clue you in for all of the *kanji* used in everyday life and beyond and can even help you remember *kanji* that you would otherwise forget. Remember radicals, from earlier? These little components are especially important to understanding stroke order without too much convolution. Simply put, each radical is written in a specific order, that order being (almost) always from left to right and from top to bottom. In the same way, *kanji* are written radical by radical, from left to right and from top to bottom. Remembering our discussion about meaning components and sound components from earlier, this means that you will write the meaning component first, as it is on the left, and then the sound component, as it is usually on the right. As is my catchphrase at this point, there are exceptions to this, such as the meaning component 辶 ("road" or "advancing"), which is usually the last radical to be written in a *kanji*, but these rules will get you through writing 90% or so of the characters in the language without trouble.

So, like how remembering radicals will help you read and understand kanji, remembering stroke order will help you remember how to write *kanji*, because it lets you see not a jumbled mess of lines and dashes, but a coherent symbol with a standard, regular way of producing one yourself that is the same as everyone else's. Proper stroke order is also a huge part of having good handwriting, as it is very hard to keep the right balance and sizing of each stroke if you are writing it haphazardly in whichever order you want. And, in the modern age, stroke order is very important when drawing a character on a touchscreen, to look up the reading of a *kanji* in a book for instance. Because of things mentioned earlier, such as the meaning component often being written first, computers will consider stroke in order to recognize the character you are drawing onto the screen. Writing with improper stroke order makes it much less likely the processor will recognize the correct character you are looking for, so it is something to be extra aware of when studying on a smartphone.

## DOTS AND DASHES: WRITING KANJI FOR YOURSELF

So that's everything. A comprehensive history of, and guide to, learning this challenging yet beautiful part of the Japanese language. If you have read this far, then you already have a considerable amount of knowledge of the many interlocking pieces that make up the form, sound, and meaning in each character, and now the only question left is: "So how do I write these on my own?"

Of course, the art of Japanese calligraphy is for some a lifelong journey to mastery, and just like master calligraphers, you won't acquire perfect handwriting overnight. However, these basic guidelines and principles will help you on the road to perfectly balanced and beautiful characters!

As with many writing systems, many kanji are very similar to one another, and their meanings can completely change based on small differences. For instance, have you ever noticed how similar a lowercase "f" and a lowercase "t" look? Like in English, rather than absolute size, these differences are recognized in the relative lengths of strokes to other ones within the character. For instance, two kanji you will encounter rather early in your study, 土 (DO, "ground") and 士 (SHI, "warrior") are differentiated only by which of the two lines are longer, as you can see. This is also the case with 未 (MI, "not yet") and 末 (MATSU, "end"), two other common characters. Luckily, the concepts represented by these kanji are all different enough that you are only rarely going to confuse someone if you accidentally write the wrong one but keeping track of the lengths of each stroke in relation to the others in each character you encounter is a quick way to start writing more balanced and precise kanji.

In a similar vein, leaving open space in some characters rather than cramming everything together is important to neat and legible handwriting. For example, 八, the character for 8, would quickly begin to resemble 入 (hai-ru, "enter") without that crucial room in the middle where the strokes are apart.

These last tips are less about accidentally writing the wrong character and more about writing characters as they are traditionally written so your handwriting doesn't look unnatural. When writing, always pay attention to which strokes run into each other, and how they intersect. When two strokes touch each other, either they intersect and one stroke pokes out from the other line, or they make a T shape with nothing jutting out.

For instance, the character 止 (to-meru, "stop") has all of its lines running up against each other, but none of them continue on past the line they touch. Compare this to the character 生 (SEI, "life"), which has many intersecting strokes. On the other hand, for strokes that do not intersect, when reaching the end of a stroke, there are 3 main ways to finish it. There is the full stop, wherein your pen or brush comes to a complete stop at the end of the line. Looking back at 止, we can see that every single stroke ends in a full stop. This is contrasted with a lingering brush line, which basically fades out as you apply less pressure over the length of the stroke. Characters with diagonal downwards lines such as 大, 人, 木, 本, etc. all use this lingering line. The last of the common ways to see strokes ended is with a curve or a hook. Hooks are more or less self-explanatory, sometimes when ending a stroke, it will hook downwards or upwards at a near-right-angle to the original line. This hook is very accentuated in kanji with the "halberd" radical, such as 戈, 式, or 代, as you can see, but it is also present in the right side of the 'hat' in 学 (GAKU, "learning").

Curved lines will be most often seen in pairs at the bottom of characters, with one going in either direction. Some examples would be 兵, 穴, and 典. In handwriting, the left curve will often be shorter and straighter, with the right curve being less angular and taking longer to fade off the page. A common variant on this two-curves-at-the-bottom pattern has a hook at the end, such as in 見 or 兄.

Now you can confidently go into the study of kanji with a large head start in the rules and traditions of the writing system. Knowledge of radicals and mnemonics gives a boost to memorization, sound components will sometimes give you a shortcut if you know how the sound component is pronounced, and your knowledge of stroke order and writing guidelines will let you learn and write beautiful characters from day one. Good luck and 頑張りましょう (try your best)!

## Part 2

# HIRAGANA AND KATAKANA CHARTS

# Hiragana Chart

This chart shows the 46 basic Hiragana with a *spelling* in Romaji for a similar phonetic sound. The vowel sounds are at the top and their counterpart versions with consonant sounds are shown below them. **note the exception 'n' - also, *wo is an uncommon kana.*

## Vowel Sounds

|   | a | i | u | e | o |
|---|---|---|---|---|---|
|   | あ a | い i | う u | え e | お o |
| k | か ka | き ki | く ku | け ke | こ ko |
| s | さ sa | し shi | す su | せ se | そ so |
| t | た ta | ち chi | つ tsu | て te | と to |
| n | な na | に ni | ぬ nu | ね ne | の no |
| h | は ha | ひ hi | ふ fu | へ he | ほ ho |
| m | ま ma | み mi | む mu | め me | も mo |
| y | や ya |   | ゆ yu |   | よ yo |
| r | ら ra | り ri | る ru | れ re | ろ ro |
| w | わ wa |   | ん **n |   | を *wo |

(Consonants)

# Modifiers

## DIACRITICS

In addition to the *basic Hiragana*, there are **25 Diacritic** symbols. These are for similar sounding syllables that are voiced differently. They are essentially the same basic symbols but with extra marks to show they should be pronounced with a slightly altered sound:

は ha — Basic

ば ba — with Dakuten

ぱ pa — with Handakuten

Basic Hiragana with these small strokes *(Dakuten)* or a circle *(Handakuten)* above them show that the consonant part of the sound needs to be changed when spoken:

- **k**-sound are pronounced with a **g**-sound.
- **s**-sounds change to a **z**-sound *(except for* し*)*.
- **t**-sounds become **d**-sounds.
- **h**-sounds become **b**-sounds with *Dakuten*.
  ...or **P**-sounds with the *Handakuten*.

|  | a | i | u | e | o |
|---|---|---|---|---|---|
| k ▸ g | が ga | ぎ gi | ぐ gu | げ ge | ご go |
| s ▸ z | ざ za | じ ji | ず zu | ぜ ze | ぞ zo |
| t ▸ d | だ da | ぢ dzi (ji) | づ dzu | で de | ど do |
| h ▸ b | ば ba | び bi | ぶ bu | べ be | ぼ bo |
| h ▸ p | ぱ pa | ぴ pi | ぷ pu | ぺ pe | ぽ po |

## DIGRAPHS

This set of symbols are called **Digraphs** - using two basic characters we have already seen, they show where two syllable sounds are combined to create a new one:

き + や = きゃ
(ki)  (ya)   (kya)

When writing these letters, it is vital that the second symbol is drawn noticeably smaller than the first. This is how we can tell that the two sounds should be combined.

Pronunciation of these so-called *compound Hiragana* sounds is quite simple - for example, き (ki) + や (ya) becomes きゃ (kya) and we pronounce it like 'kiya' *without the 'i' sound.*

Don't let the chart below scare you - all of the Digraphs are made *exclusively* with letters from the い/i column *(excluding itself)* **and** they are only modified by letters from row **Y**!

| きゃ | きゅ | きょ | ぎゃ | ぎゅ | ぎょ |
|---|---|---|---|---|---|
| kya | kyu | kyo | gya | gyu | gyo |
| しゃ | しゅ | しょ | じゃ | じゅ | じょ |
| sha | shu | sho | ja | ju | jo |
| ちゃ | ちゅ | ちょ | にゃ | にゅ | にょ |
| cha | chu | cho | nya | nyu | nyo |
| ひゃ | ひゅ | ひょ | びゃ | びゅ | びょ |
| hya | hyu | hyo | bya | byu | byo |
| ぴゃ | ぴゅ | ぴょ | りゃ | りゅ | りょ |
| pya | pyu | pyo | rya | ryu | ryo |
| みゃ | みゅ | みょ | | | |
| mya | myu | myo | | | |

Modifiers

# Modifiers

## DOUBLE CONSONANTS

We also need to be aware that some Japanese words contain a *double consonant sound*. When writing these words, we add an extra symbol in the form of a small つ/**tsu** *(called sokuon)* to show that it needs to be pronounced differently. Let's look at an example:

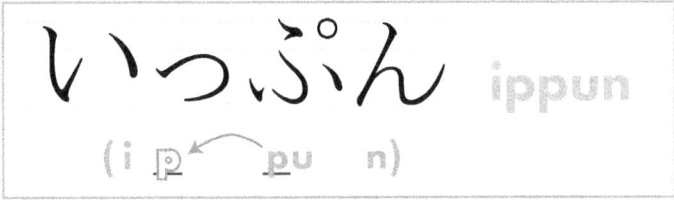

Without the small つ *(tsu)*, the word いぷん *(ipun)* doesn't have any meaning but いっぷん *(ippun)*, with the *sokuon*, means (a) minute.

Notice that the small つ is placed **before** the character that it takes the extra consonant sound from. When you see words with this modifier, the consonant part of the symbol that follows it *(in this example, the 'p' from 'pu')* is added to the end of the sound before it.

Both consonants need to be heard separately when the word is spoken, like saying **'ip-pun'** but without leaving a gap than can be heard.

## LONG VOWEL SOUNDS

Just as there are double consonant sounds, we need to be aware of elongated vowel sounds too *(e.g. aa, ii. oo, ee, and uu)*. When speaking, we simply extend the duration of the sound (usually double) but in writing these words, the long vowel sound is shown with an additional character *(called a chouon)*. The character used varies depending on the vowel:

| Vowel | Extender |
|---|---|
| a | あ |
| i / e | い |
| u / o | う |

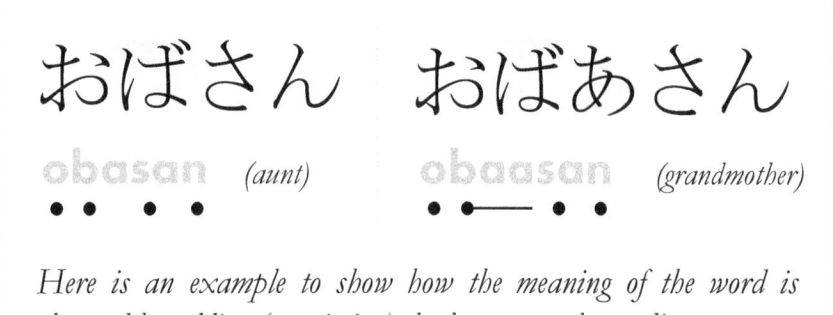

*Here is an example to show how the meaning of the word is changed by adding (or missing) the longer vowel sound!*

*The Japanese language is full of exceptions but they tend to be learned with experience. It's just useful to be aware of double consonants and vowels for now, so you can understand when you see one!*

# Katakana Chart

This chart shows the 46 basic Katakana with a *spelling* in Romaji for a similar phonetic sound. The vowel sounds are at the top and their counterpart versions with consonant sounds are shown below them. **note the exception 'n' - also, *wo is an uncommon kana.*

Vowel Sounds

|   | a | i | u | e | o |
|---|---|---|---|---|---|
|   | ア a | イ i | ウ u | エ e | オ o |
| k | カ ka | キ ki | ク ku | ケ ke | コ ko |
| s | サ sa | シ shi | ス su | セ se | ソ so |
| t | タ ta | チ chi | ツ tsu | テ te | ト to |
| n | ナ na | ニ ni | ヌ nu | ネ ne | ノ no |
| h | ハ ha | ヒ hi | フ fu | ヘ he | ホ ho |
| m | マ ma | ミ mi | ム mu | メ me | モ mo |
| y | ヤ ya |   | ユ yu |   | ヨ yo |
| r | ラ ra | リ ri | ル ru | レ re | ロ ro |
| w | ワ wa |   | ン **n |   | ヲ *wo |

Consonants

Lorem ipsum

# Modifiers

## DIACRITICS

Just as with *Hiragana*, there are **25 Diacritic** symbols in **Katakana**. They are used in the same way, to show when similar sounding syllables need to be voiced differently. Even more conveniently, the marks to show this change in sound are identical:

| Basic | with Dakuten | with Handakuten |

The rules for Katakana diacritic symbols work the same way. *Dakuten* and *Handakuten* show us that the consonant part of the sound needs to be changed when spoken:

- **k**-sound are pronounced with a **g**-sound.
- **s**-sounds change to a **z**-sound *(except for し)*.
- **t**-sounds become **d**-sounds.
- **h**-sounds become **b**-sounds with *Dakuten*.
  ...or **P**-sounds with the *Handakuten*.

|  | a | i | u | e | o |
|---|---|---|---|---|---|
| k ▸ g | ガ ga | ギ gi | グ gu | ゲ ge | ゴ go |
| s ▸ z | ザ za | ジ ji | ズ zu | ゼ ze | ゾ zo |
| t ▸ d | ダ da | ヂ dzi (ji) | ヅ dzu | デ de | ド do |
| h ▸ b | バ ba | ビ bi | ブ bu | ベ be | ボ bo |
| h ▸ p | パ pa | ピ pi | プ pu | ペ pe | ポ po |

Modifiers

## DIGRAPHS

Here are the **Digraphs** for Katakana too - once more, we use two basic characters to show where two syllable sounds are combined to make another one. *Easy, right?*

キ + ヤ = キャ
(ki)  (ya)    (kya)

The characters used have the same sounds as the two corresponding Hiragana. The importance of writing the second symbol smaller than the first still applies.

Pronunciation of these so-called *compound Katakana* sounds is just as simple - for example, キ (ki) + ヤ (ya) becomes キャ (kya) and we pronounce it as 'kiya' *without the 'i' sound.*

This table looks complex but just remember that Digraphs are made *exclusively* with letters from the イ/i column *(excluding itself)* **and** modified by letters from row **Y**!

| キャ | キュ | キョ | ギャ | ギュ | ギョ |
|---|---|---|---|---|---|
| kya | kyu | kyo | gya | gyu | gyo |
| シャ | シュ | ショ | ジャ | ジュ | ジョ |
| sha | shu | sho | ja | ju | jo |
| チャ | チュ | チョ | ニャ | ニュ | ニョ |
| cha | chu | cho | nya | nyu | nyo |
| ニャ | ヒュ | ヒョ | ビャ | ビュ | ビョ |
| hya | hyu | hyo | bya | byu | byo |
| ピャ | ピュ | ピョ | リャ | リュ | リョ |
| pya | pyu | pyo | rya | ryu | ryo |
| ミャ | ミュ | ミョ | | | |
| mya | myu | myo | | | |

Modifiers

# Modifiers

## DOUBLE CONSONANTS

Japanese words with Katakana can contain a *double consonant sound* too. These words also feature the small ツ / **tsu** *(called sokuon)* to show that it should be pronounced differently. Let's look at another example for Katakana:

ペット *petto*
( pe t to )

Without the small ツ *(tsu)*, the word ペト *(peto)* doesn't have any meaning but ペット *(petto)*, with the *sokuon*, means **pet** - like a hamster or cat!

Notice that the small ツ is placed **before** the character that it takes the extra consonant sound from. When you see words with this modifier, the consonant part of the symbol that follows it *(in this example, the 't' from 'to')* is added to the end of the sound before it.

Both consonants need to be heard separately when the word is spoken, like saying **'pet-to'** but without leaving a gap than can be heard.

## LONG VOWEL SOUNDS

We still need to be aware of elongated vowel sounds *(e.g. aa, ii, oo, ee, and uu)*. When spoken, the duration of the sound is extended (usually double again) but when written in Katakana we use a line ー *(called 伸ばし棒, which literally means 'stretching bar')*.

This is one way Katakana differs from Hiragana, aside from the shapes, as that uses an additional vowel symbol to denote a long vowel sound. Let's look at some examples:

フ + リ = フリー　　ケ + キ = ケーキ
(fu) (ri) — fu-rii *(free)*　　(ke) — (ki) kee-ki *(cake)*

*It is worth noting that the 'stretching bar' is rotated to a vertical line when text is written vertically.*

## Part 3

# STROKE ORDER DIAGRAMS

| KANJI # | RADICAL | STROKES | MEANING | UNICODE |
|---|---|---|---|---|
| 0012 | 日 | 4 | day, sun, Japan, counter for days | 65E5 |

**ONYOMI**

ニチ、ジツ

*nichi, jitsu*

**KUNYOMI**

ひ、-び、-か

*hi, -bi, -ka*

**VOCABULARY**

| | | | |
|---|---|---|---|
| 毎日(まいにち) | every day | 明日(あした) | tomorrow |
| 今日 (きょう) | today | 休日（きゅうじつ） | day off |
| 昨日(きのう) | yesterday | 日曜日(にちようび) | sunday |

## STROKE ORDER

How this Kanji is drawn

## PRACTICE

Trace and practice this Kanji below

STYLES

| KANJI # | RADICAL | STROKES | MEANING | | UNICODE |
|---|---|---|---|---|---|
| **0001** | 一 | 1 | **one** | | **4E00** |

| | ONYOMI | KUNYOMI |
|---|---|---|
| | **イチ** | **ひと(つ)** |
| | *ichi* | *hito(tsu)* |

**VOCABULARY**

| | | | |
|---|---|---|---|
| 一〇〇 (ひゃく) | one hundred | 一番 (いちばん) | first place |
| 一人(ひとり) | one person | 一度(いちど) | once |
| 一緒に(いっしょ) | together(with) | | |

## STROKE ORDER
How this Kanji is drawn

## PRACTICE
Trace and practice this Kanji below

STYLES

| KANJI # | RADICAL | STROKES | MEANING | | | UNICODE |
|---|---|---|---|---|---|---|
| 0624 | 口 | 8 | country | | | 56FD |

**ONYOMI**
コク
*koku*

**KUNYOMI**
くに
*kuni*

**VOCABULARY**

| 国家 (こっか) | state | 外国 (がいこく) | foreign country |
|---|---|---|---|
| 国際 (こくさい) | international | 全国 (ぜんこく) | countrywide |
| 国籍 (こくせき) | nationality | 国土 (こくど) | country |

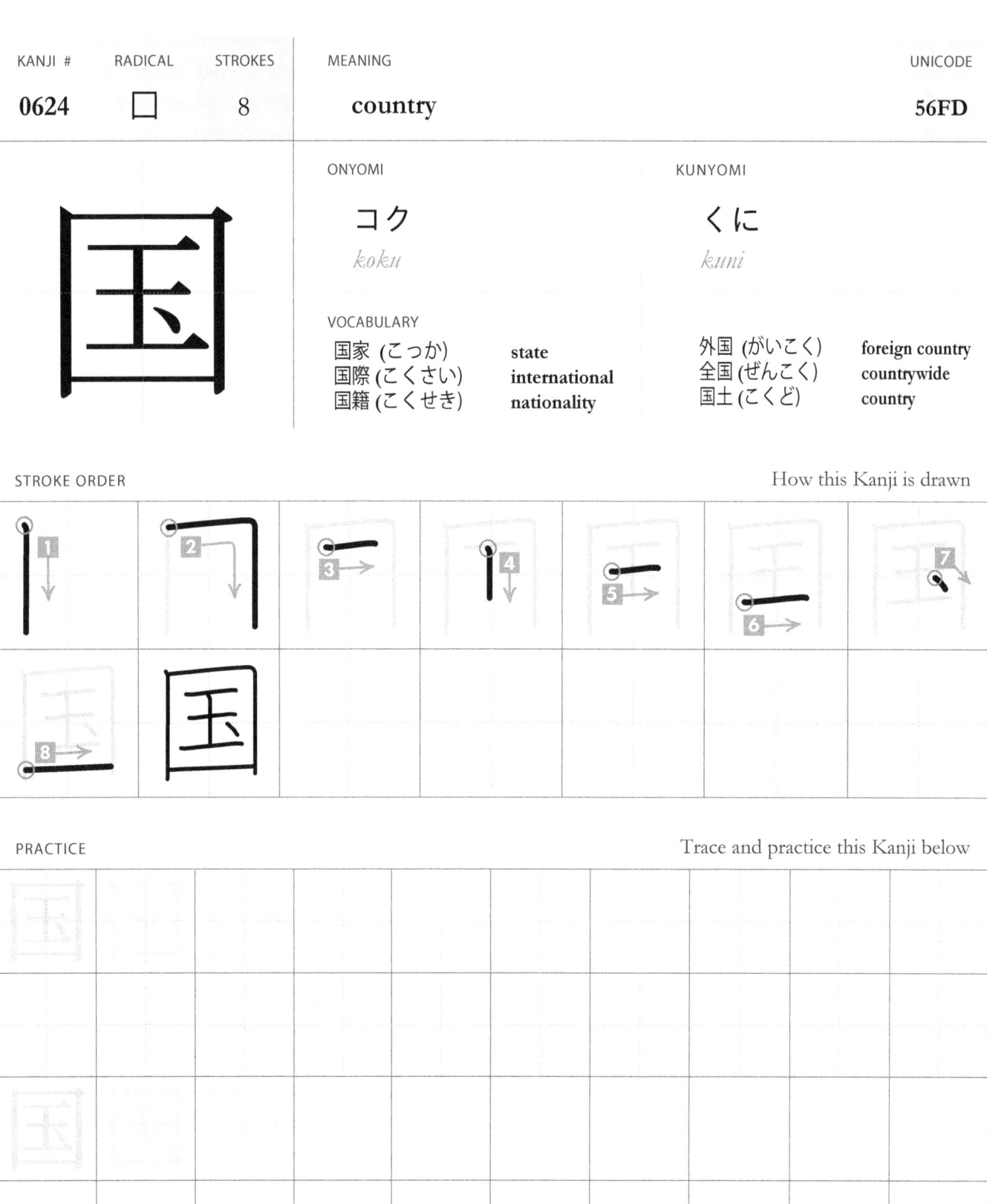

**STROKE ORDER** — How this Kanji is drawn

**PRACTICE** — Trace and practice this Kanji below

**STYLES**

| KANJI # | RADICAL | STROKES | MEANING | | UNICODE |
|---------|---------|---------|---------|---|---------|
| 0012 | 人 | 2 | person | | 4EBA |

**ONYOMI**
ジン、ニン
*jin, nin*

**KUNYOMI**
ひと
*hito*

**VOCABULARY**

| 人生 (じんせい) | life | 二人 (ふたり) | two people |
| 人口 (じんこう) | population | 犯人 (はんにん) | offender |
| 人類 (じんるい) | mankind | 友人 (ゆうじん) | friend |

## STROKE ORDER
*How this Kanji is drawn*

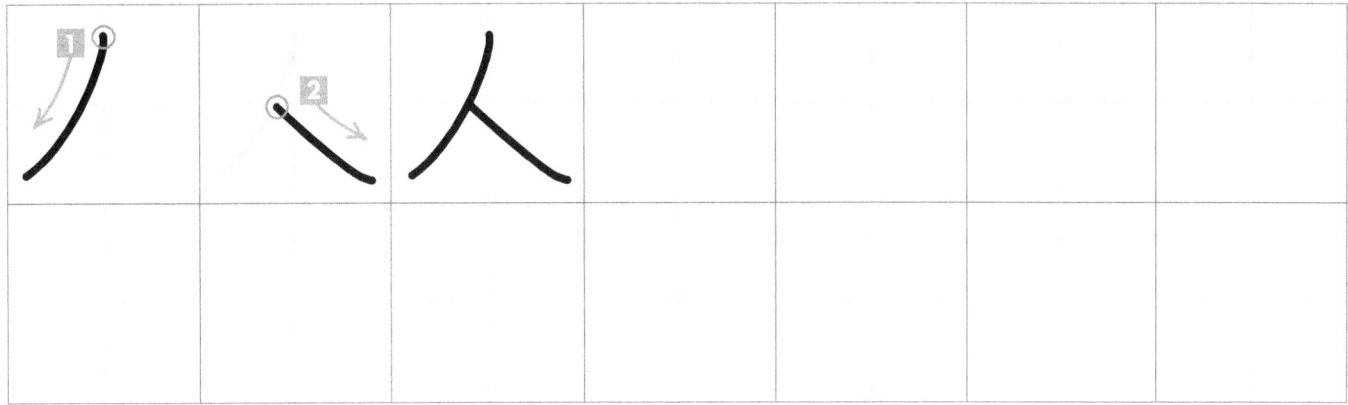

## PRACTICE
*Trace and practice this Kanji below*

## STYLES

| KANJI # | RADICAL | STROKES | MEANING | | UNICODE |
|---|---|---|---|---|---|
| 1114 | 干 | 6 | year, counter for years | | 5E74 |

## 年

**ONYOMI**
ネン
*nen*

**KUNYOMI**
とし
*toshi*

**VOCABULARY**

| | | | | |
|---|---|---|---|---|
| 年齢 (ねんれい) | age; years | | 毎年 (まいとし) | every year |
| 年月 (としつき) | month and years | | 今年 (ことし) | this year |
| 年金 (ねんきん) | annuity; pension | | 来年 (らいねん) | next year |

**STROKE ORDER** — How this Kanji is drawn

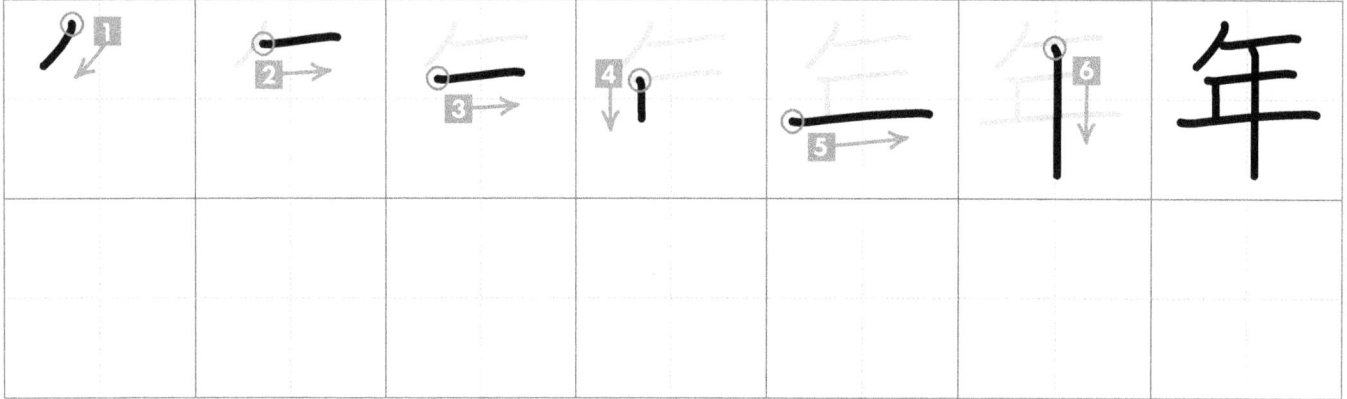

**PRACTICE** — Trace and practice this Kanji below

**STYLES** 年 年 年 年 年 年 年 年

| KANJI # | RADICAL | STROKES | MEANING | UNICODE |
|---|---|---|---|---|
| 0112 | 大 | 3 | large, big | 5927 |

**ONYOMI**
ダイ、タイ
*dai, tai*

**KUNYOMI**
おお(きい)
*oo(kii)*

**VOCABULARY**

| | | | |
|---|---|---|---|
| 大人 (おとな) | adult | 肥大 (ひだい) | swell; enlarge |
| 大きい (おお) | big; large | 特大 (とくだい) | extra large |
| 大会 (たいかい) | convention | 絶大 (ぜつだい) | tremendous |

## STROKE ORDER
*How this Kanji is drawn*

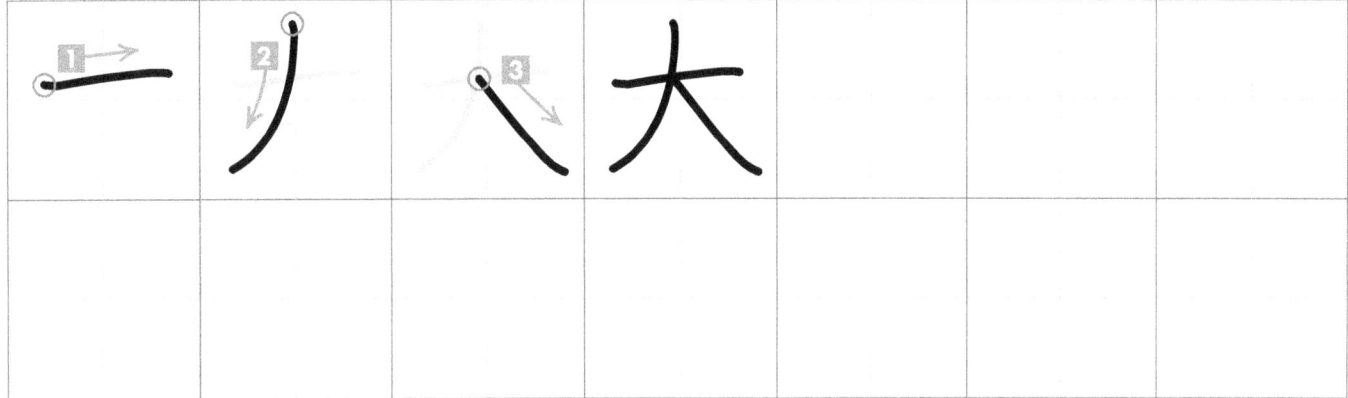

## PRACTICE
*Trace and practice this Kanji below*

## STYLES

| KANJI # | RADICAL | STROKES | MEANING | | UNICODE |
|---------|---------|---------|---------|---|---------|
| 0010 | 十 | 2 | ten, 10 | | 5341 |

**ONYOMI**  
ジュウ  
*juu*

**KUNYOMI**  
とお、と  
*tou, to*

**VOCABULARY**

| | | | |
|---|---|---|---|
| 十分 (じゅうぶん) | plenty; enough | 七十 (ななじゅう) | seventy |
| 十時 (じゅうじ) | 10 o'clock | 十一 (じゅういち) | eleven |
| 十月 (じゅうがつ) | October | 十人 (じゅうにん) | ten people |

## STROKE ORDER
*How this Kanji is drawn*

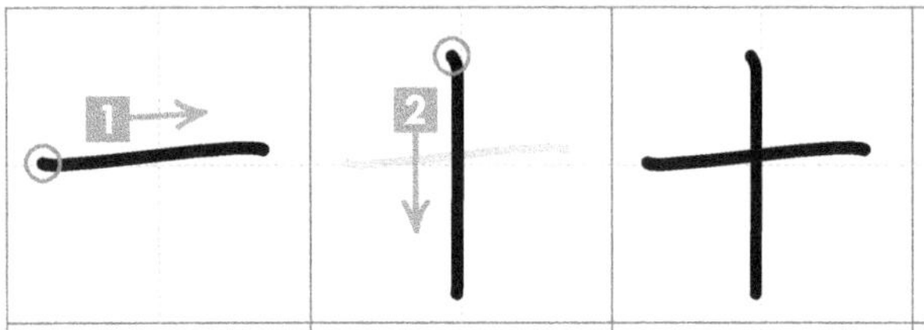

## PRACTICE
*Trace and practice this Kanji below*

STYLES

| KANJI # | RADICAL | STROKES | MEANING | UNICODE |
|---|---|---|---|---|
| 0012 | 二 | 2 | two, 2 | 4E8C |

**ONYOMI**

二、ジ
*ni, ji*

**KUNYOMI**

ふた(つ)、ふたたび
*futa(tsu), futatabi*

**VOCABULARY**

| | | | |
|---|---|---|---|
| 二つ (ふた) | two | 十二 (じゅうに) | twelve |
| 二人 (ふたり) | two persons | 無二 (むに) | peerless; matchless |
| 二時 (にじ) | two o'clock | 第二 (だいに) | second |

## STROKE ORDER
*How this Kanji is drawn*

## PRACTICE
*Trace and practice this Kanji below*

## STYLES

| KANJI # | RADICAL | STROKES | MEANING | UNICODE |
|---|---|---|---|---|
| 0224 | 木 | 5 | book, present, true, counter for long cylinders | 672C |

**ONYOMI**
ホン
*hon*

**KUNYOMI**
もと
*moto*

**VOCABULARY**

本来 (ほんらい) — originally; primarily
本名 (ほんみょう) — real name
本日 (ほんじつ) — today

日本 (にほん) — Japan
基本 (きほん) — foundation; basis
手本 (てほん) — copybook

## STROKE ORDER
How this Kanji is drawn

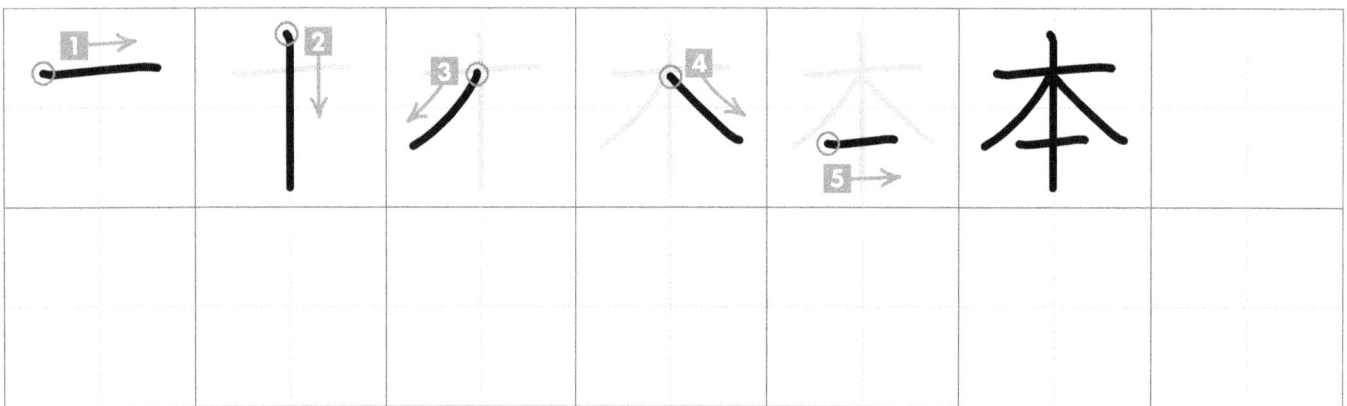

## PRACTICE
Trace and practice this Kanji below

STYLES 本 本 本 本 本 本 本 本

| KANJI # | RADICAL | STROKES | MEANING | UNICODE |
|---|---|---|---|---|
| 0039 | 丨 | 4 | in, inside, middle, mean, center | 4E2D |

**中**

**ONYOMI**
チュウ
*chuu*

**KUNYOMI**
なか、うち、あた(る)
*naka, uchi, ata(ru)*

**VOCABULARY**

中国 (ちゅうごく) China
中止 (ちゅうし) suspension
中身 (なかみ) contents

途中 (とちゅう) on the way
集中 (しゅうちゅう) concentration
市中 (しちゅう) in the city

## STROKE ORDER
How this Kanji is drawn

## PRACTICE
Trace and practice this Kanji below

## STYLES

| KANJI # | RADICAL | STROKES | MEANING | UNICODE |
|---|---|---|---|---|
| 2070 | 長 | 8 | long, leader, superior, senior | 9577 |

**ONYOMI**
チョウ
*chou*

**KUNYOMI**
なが(い)、おさ
*naga(i), osa*

**VOCABULARY**

長年 (ながねん) — long time
長期 (ちょうき) — long-term
長所 (ちょうしょ) — strong point

社長 (しゃちょう) — company president
全長 (ぜんちょう) — overall length
機長 (きちょう) — pilot

**STROKE ORDER** — How this Kanji is drawn

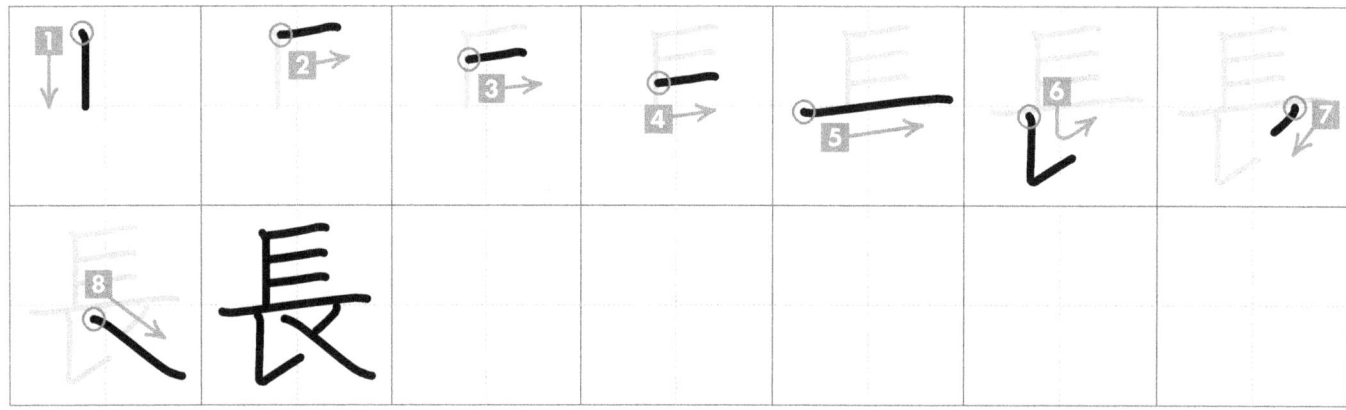

**PRACTICE** — Trace and practice this Kanji below

STYLES

| KANJI # | RADICAL | STROKES | MEANING | UNICODE |
|---|---|---|---|---|
| 0829 | 凵 | 5 | **exit, leave, go out** | 51FA |

| ONYOMI | KUNYOMI |
|---|---|
| シュツ、スイ | で(る)、だ(す)、い(でる) |
| *shutsu, sui* | *de(ru), da(su), i(deru)* |

**VOCABULARY**

出発 (しゅっぱつ) departure
出口 (でぐち) exit
出版 (しゅっぱん) publication
見出し (みだ) heading
演出 (えんしゅつ) production
出来事 (できごと) incident

**STROKE ORDER** — How this Kanji is drawn

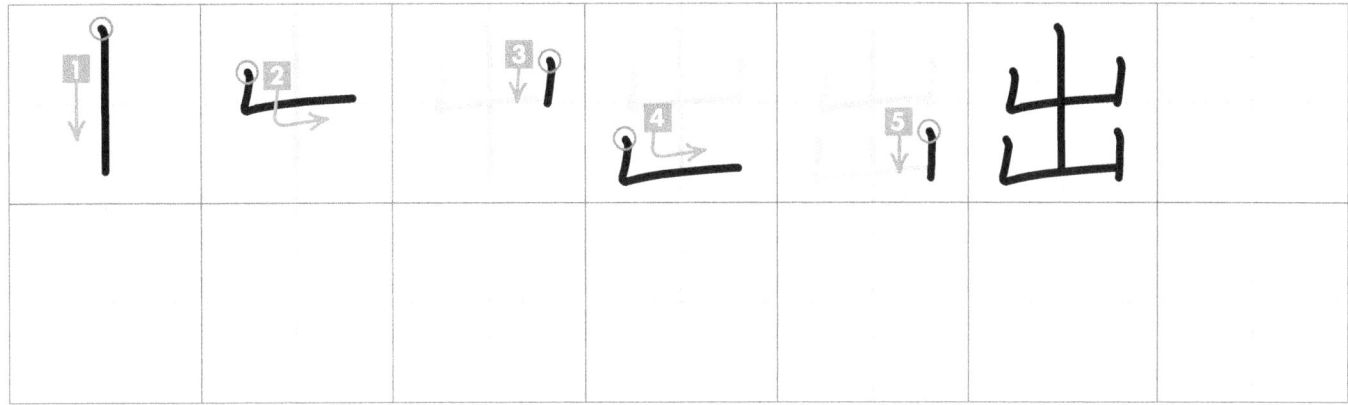

**PRACTICE** — Trace and practice this Kanji below

**STYLES**

出 出 出 出 出 出 出 出

37

| KANJI # | RADICAL | STROKES | MEANING | | UNICODE |
|---|---|---|---|---|---|
| 0003 | 一 | 3 | three, 3 | | 4E09 |

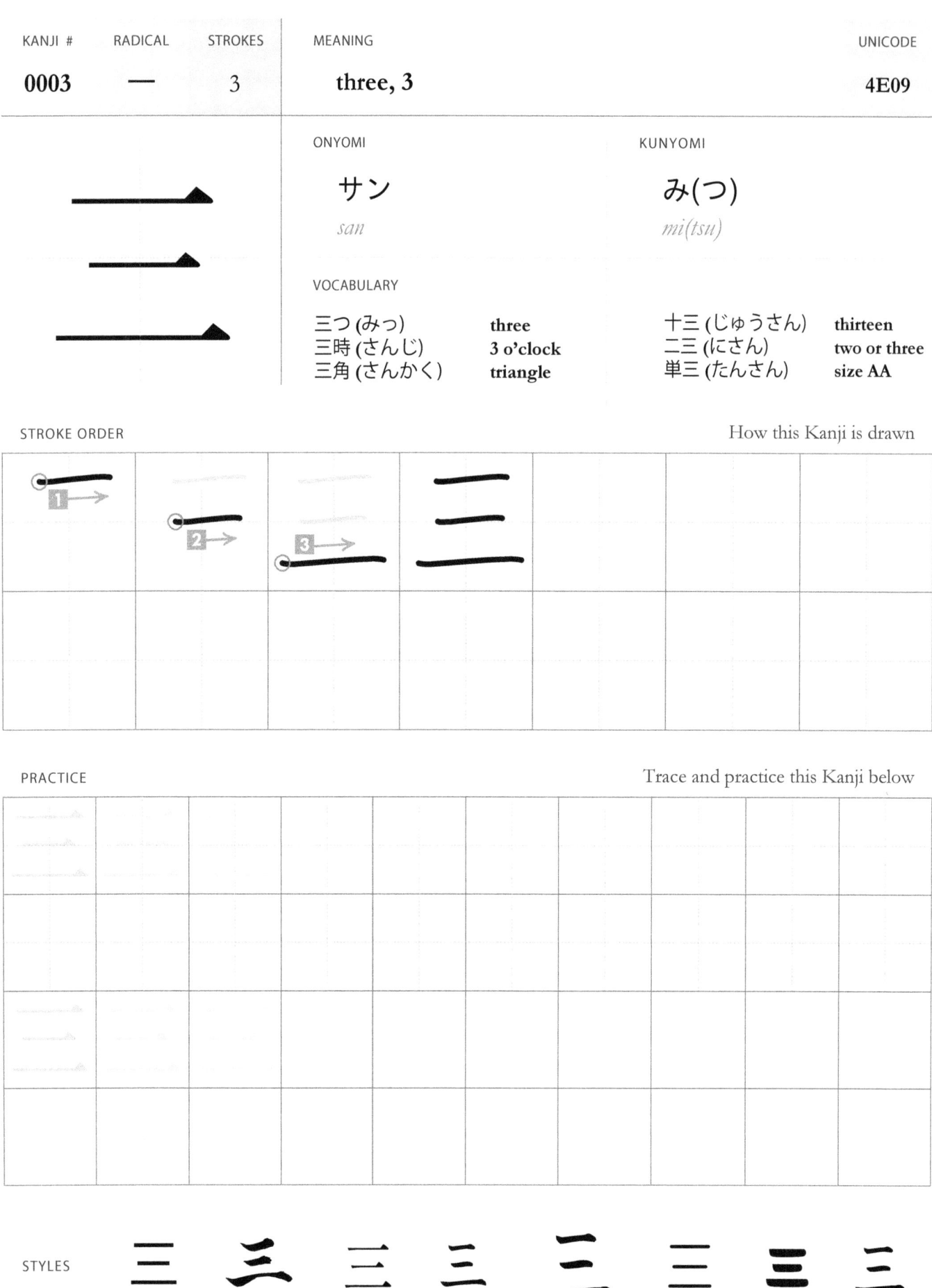

ONYOMI

サン
*san*

KUNYOMI

み(つ)
*mi(tsu)*

VOCABULARY

| 三つ (みっ) | three | 十三 (じゅうさん) | thirteen |
| 三時 (さんじ) | 3 o'clock | 二三 (にさん) | two or three |
| 三角 (さんかく) | triangle | 単三 (たんさん) | size AA |

STROKE ORDER — How this Kanji is drawn

PRACTICE — Trace and practice this Kanji below

STYLES

38

| KANJI # | RADICAL | STROKES | MEANING | | UNICODE |
|---|---|---|---|---|---|
| 0171 | 日 | 10 | time, hour | | 6642 |

**ONYOMI**
ジ
*ji*

**KUNYOMI**
とき、-どき
*toki, doki*

**VOCABULARY**

| | | | |
|---|---|---|---|
| 時計 (とけい) | watch; clock | 日時 (にちじ) | date and time |
| 時半 (じはん) | about an hour | 何時 (いつ) | when; how soon |
| 時差 (じさ) | time difference | 同時 (どうじ) | simultaneously |

## STROKE ORDER — How this Kanji is drawn

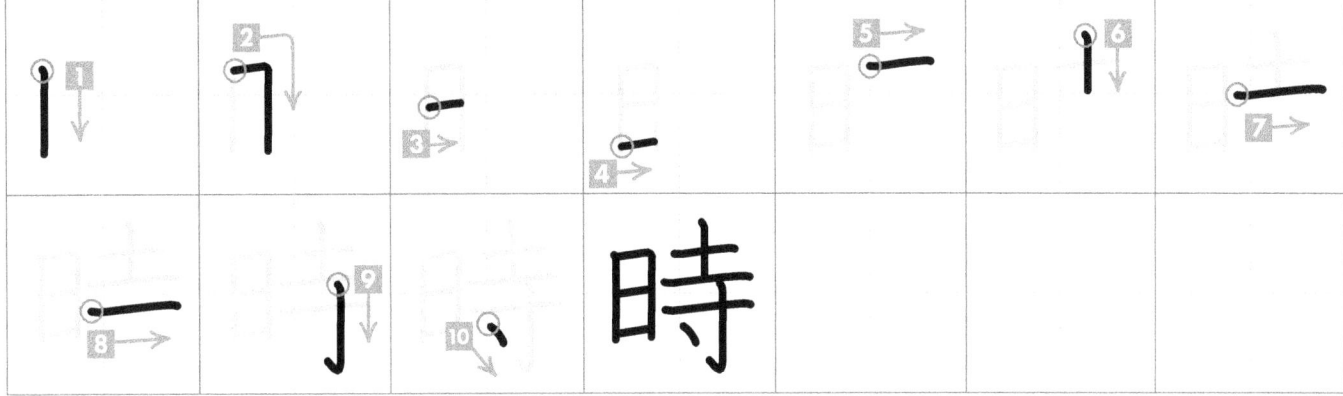

## PRACTICE — Trace and practice this Kanji below

## STYLES

時 時 時 時 時 時 時 時

| KANJI # | RADICAL | STROKES | MEANING | UNICODE |
|---|---|---|---|---|
| 0938 | 行 | 6 | going, journey, carry out, line, row | 884C |

**ONYOMI**
コウ、ギョウ、アン
*kou, gyou, an*

**KUNYOMI**
い(く)、ゆ(く)、おこな(う)
*i(ku), yu(ku), okona(u)*

**VOCABULARY**

| | | | |
|---|---|---|---|
| 行き (ゆ) | bound for | 旅行 (りょこう) | travel; trip |
| 行事 (ぎょうじ) | event; function | 銀行 (ぎんこう) | bank |
| 行政 (ぎょうせい) | administration | 流行 (りゅうこう) | fashion |

## STROKE ORDER
*How this Kanji is drawn*

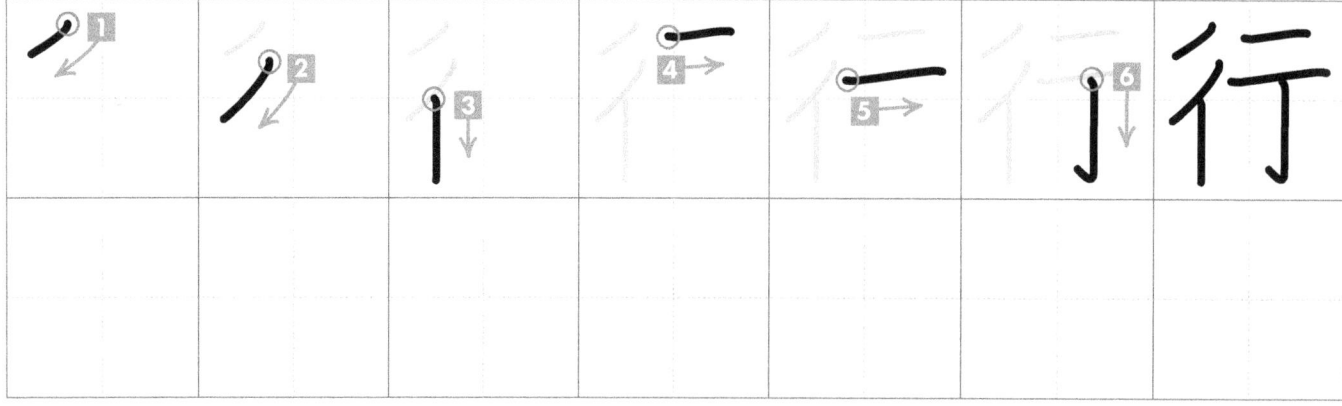

## PRACTICE
*Trace and practice this Kanji below*

| KANJI # | RADICAL | STROKES | MEANING | UNICODE |
|---|---|---|---|---|
| 0061 | 見 | 7 | see, hopes, chances, idea, opinion, look at | 898B |

**ONYOMI**

ケン
*ken*

**KUNYOMI**

み(る)、み(せる)
*mi(ru), mi(seru)*

**VOCABULARY**

| | | | |
|---|---|---|---|
| 見る (み) | to see; to look | 発見 (はっけん) | discovery |
| 見出し (みだ) | heading | 一見 (いっけん) | look; glimpse |
| 見解 (けんかい) | opinion | 会見 (かいけん) | interview |

**STROKE ORDER** — How this Kanji is drawn

**PRACTICE** — Trace and practice this Kanji below

**STYLES**

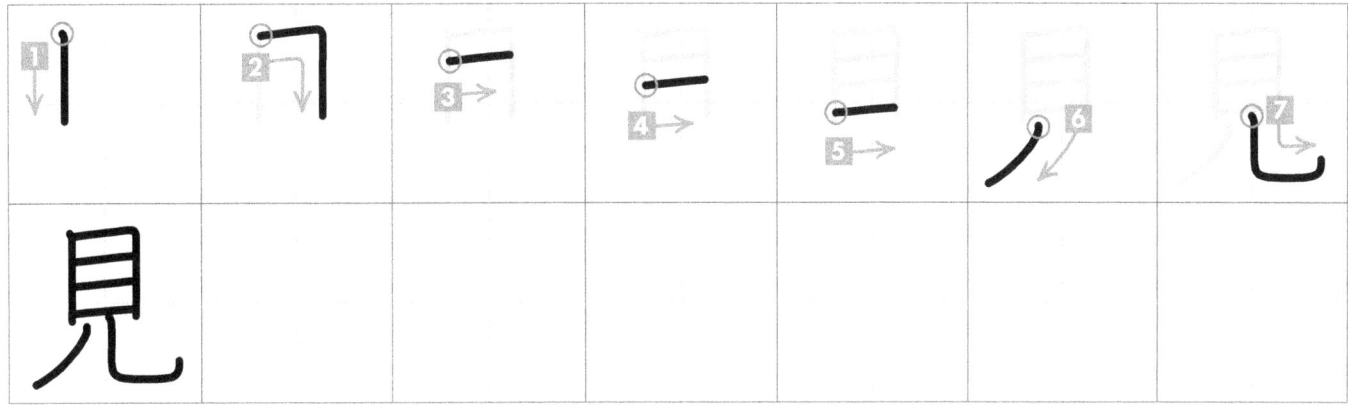

| KANJI # | RADICAL | STROKES | MEANING | UNICODE |
|---|---|---|---|---|
| 0013 | 日 | 4 | **month, moon** | 6708 |

**ONYOMI**
ゲツ、ガツ
*getsu, gatsu*

**KUNYOMI**
つき
*tsuki*

**VOCABULARY**

| | | | | |
|---|---|---|---|---|
| 月曜 (げつよう) | Monday | 毎月 (まいつき) | every month |
| 月日 (つきひ) | time; years; days | 今月 (こんげつ) | this month |
| 月給 (げっきゅう) | monthly salary | 来月 (らいげつ) | next month |

## STROKE ORDER
*How this Kanji is drawn*

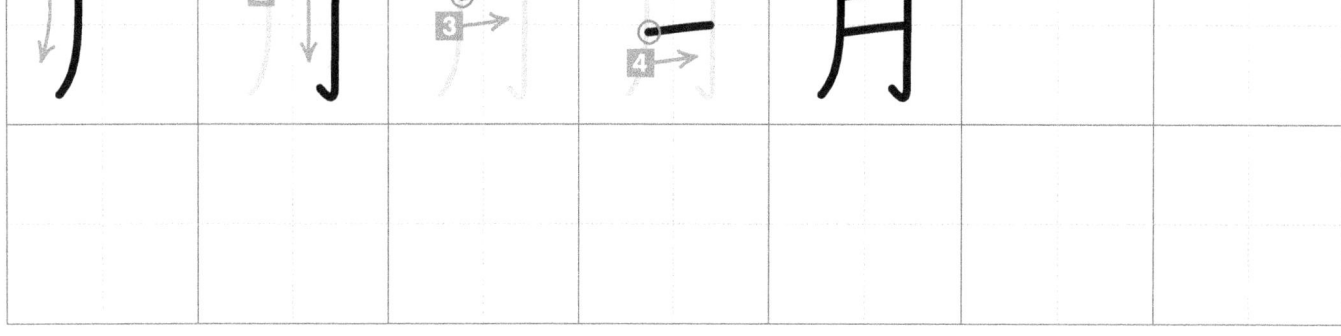

## PRACTICE
*Trace and practice this Kanji below*

STYLES

| KANJI # | RADICAL | STROKES | MEANING | UNICODE |
|---|---|---|---|---|
| 0844 | 刀 | 4 | part, minute of time, understand | 5206 |

**ONYOMI**
ブン、フン、ブ
*bun, fun, bu*

**KUNYOMI**
わ(ける)
*wa(keru)*

**VOCABULARY**

| | | | | |
|---|---|---|---|---|
| 分かる (わ) | to understand | 半分 (はんぶん) | half |
| 分野 (ぶんや) | field; sphere | 自分 (じぶん) | myself; yourself |
| 分析 (ぶんせき) | analysis | 気分 (きぶん) | feeling; mood |

## STROKE ORDER
*How this Kanji is drawn*

## PRACTICE
*Trace and practice this Kanji below*

## STYLES

43

| KANJI # | RADICAL | STROKES | MEANING | UNICODE |
|---|---|---|---|---|
| 1479 | 彳 | 9 | behind, back, later | 5F8C |

### ONYOMI
ゴ、コウ
*go, kou*

### KUNYOMI
のち、うし(ろ)、あと
*nochi, ushi(ro), ato*

### VOCABULARY

| | | | |
|---|---|---|---|
| 後ろ (うし) | back; behind | 今後 (こんご) | from now on |
| 後半 (こうはん) | second half | 午後 (ごご) | afternoon; p.m. |
| 後で (あと) | afterwards | 前後 (ぜんご) | front and rear |

### STROKE ORDER — How this Kanji is drawn

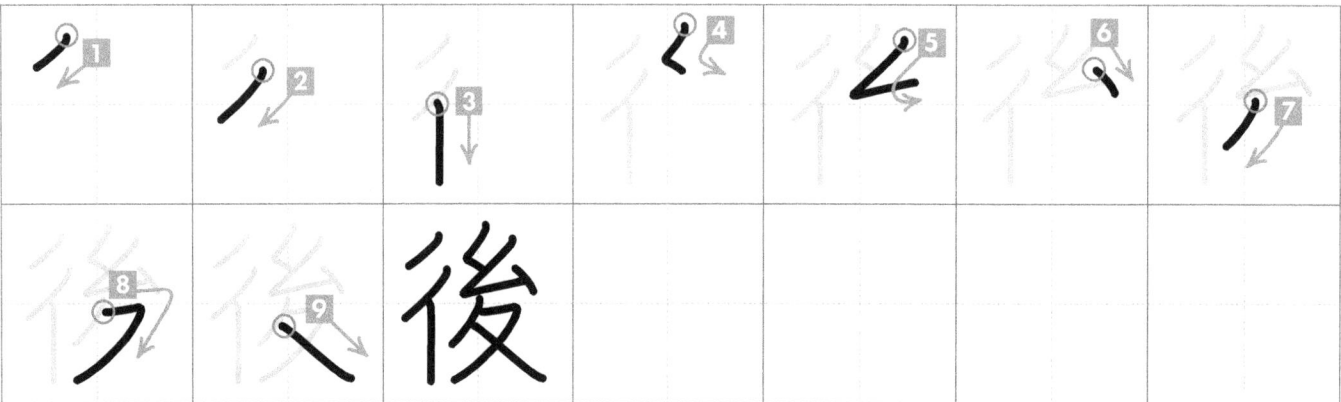

### PRACTICE — Trace and practice this Kanji below

### STYLES

後 後 後 後 後 後 後

| KANJI # | RADICAL | STROKES | MEANING | UNICODE |
|---|---|---|---|---|
| 0309 | 刀 | 9 | in front, before | 524D |

**ONYOMI**  
ゼン  
*zen*

**KUNYOMI**  
まえ  
*mae*

**VOCABULARY**

| | | | |
|---|---|---|---|
| 前半 (ぜんはん) | first half | 名前 (なまえ) | name; full name |
| 前進 (ぜんしん) | advance; drive | 午前 (ごぜん) | morning; A.M. |
| 前日 (ぜんじつ) | previous day | 出前 (でまえ) | catering; home delivery |

## STROKE ORDER — How this Kanji is drawn

## PRACTICE — Trace and practice this Kanji below

## STYLES

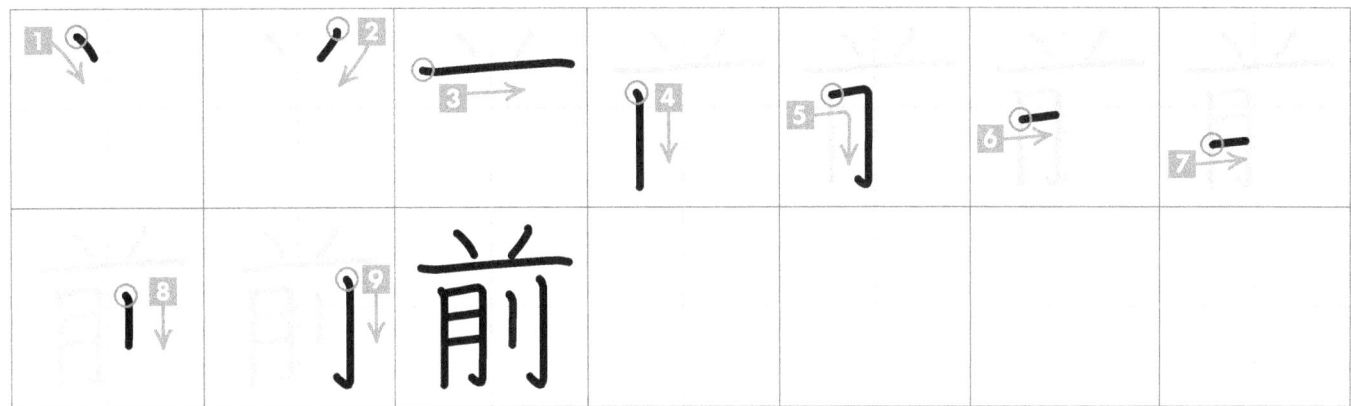

| KANJI # | RADICAL | STROKES | MEANING | | UNICODE |
|---|---|---|---|---|---|
| 1675 | 生 | 5 | life, genuine, birth | | 751F |

生

**ONYOMI**
セイ、ショウ
*sei, shou*

**KUNYOMI** い(きる), う(む)、お(う)、は(える)、なま
*i(kiru), u(mu), o(u), ha(eru), nama*

**VOCABULARY**

| | | | |
|---|---|---|---|
| 生徒 (せいと) | pupil | 学生 (がくせい) | student |
| 生きる (い) | to live; to exist | 先生 (せんせい)) | teacher; master |
| 生命 (せいめい) | life; existance | 一生 (いっしょう) | whole life |

## STROKE ORDER
How this Kanji is drawn

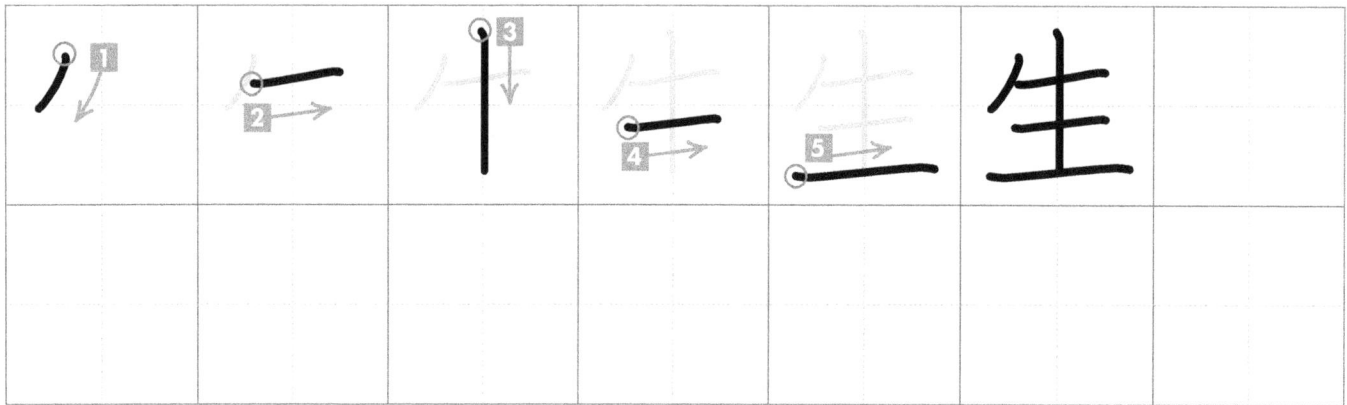

## PRACTICE
Trace and practice this Kanji below

STYLES   生 生 生 生 生 生 生 生

46

| KANJI # | RADICAL | STROKES | MEANING | | UNICODE |
|---|---|---|---|---|---|
| 0005 | 二 | 4 | **five, 5** | | 4E94 |

## 五

**ONYOMI**
ゴ
*go*

**KUNYOMI**
いつ(つ)
*itsu(tsu)*

**VOCABULARY**

| | | | |
|---|---|---|---|
| 五日 (いつか) | five days | 十五 (じゅうご) | fifteen |
| 五時 (ごじ) | five o'clock | 単五 (たんご) | size N (battery) |
| 五百 (ごひゃく) | 500 | 第五 (だいご) | the fifth |

## STROKE ORDER
*How this Kanji is drawn*

## PRACTICE
*Trace and practice this Kanji below*

## STYLES
五 五 五 五 五 五 五 五

| KANJI # | RADICAL | STROKES | MEANING | UNICODE |
|---|---|---|---|---|
| 1747 | 門 | 12 | **interval, space** | 9593 |

**ONYOMI**
カン、ケン
*kan, ken*

**KUNYOMI**
あいだ、ま、あい
*aida, ma, ai*

**VOCABULARY**

| | | | |
|---|---|---|---|
| 間接 (かんせつ) | indirection | 人間 (にんげん) | human being |
| 間隔 (かんかく) | space; interval | 期間 (きかん) | period; term |
| 間近 (まぢか) | proximity; nearness | 世間 (せけん) | world; society |

**STROKE ORDER** — How this Kanji is drawn

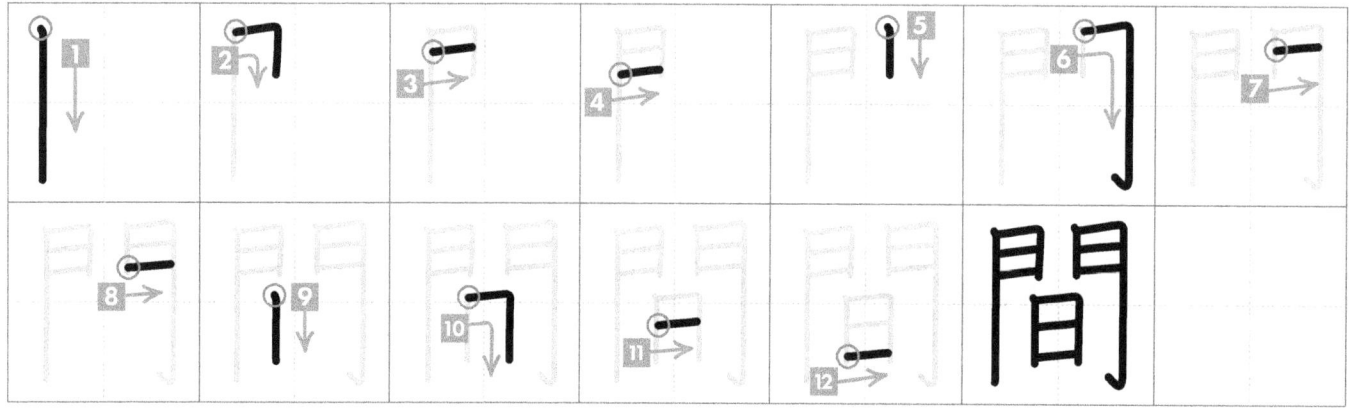

**PRACTICE** — Trace and practice this Kanji below

**STYLES** 間 間 間 間 間 間 間 間

| KANJI # | RADICAL | STROKES | MEANING | UNICODE |
|---|---|---|---|---|
| 0050 | 一 | 3 | **above, up** | 4E0A |

ONYOMI ジョウ、ショウ、シャン

*jou, shou, shan*

KUNYOMI うえ、うわ-
うえ、うわ-、かみ、あ(げる)、のぼ(る)、たてまつ(る)

*ue, uwa, kami, a(geru), nobo(ru), tatematsu(ru)*

**VOCABULARY**

| | | | |
|---|---|---|---|
| 上下 (じょうげ) | top and bottom | 以上 (いじょう) | not less than |
| 上り (のぼ) | ascent; climbing | 屋上 (おくじょう) | rooftop |
| 上る (のぼ) | to ascend; to go up | 年上 (としうえ) | older; senior |

**STROKE ORDER**  How this Kanji is drawn

**PRACTICE**  Trace and practice this Kanji below

**STYLES**  上 上 上 上 上 上 上 上

| KANJI # | RADICAL | STROKES | MEANING | UNICODE |
|---|---|---|---|---|
| 0543 | 木 | 8 | east | 6771 |

東

**ONYOMI**
トウ
*tou*

**KUNYOMI**
ひがし
*higashi*

**VOCABULARY**

| | | | | |
|---|---|---|---|---|
| 東西 (とうざい) | east and west | 北東 (ほくとう) | northeast |
| 東洋 (とうよう) | Orient | 南東 (なんとう) | southeast |
| 東北 (とうほく) | north-east; Tohoku | 東京 (とうきょう) | Tokyo |

## STROKE ORDER
*How this Kanji is drawn*

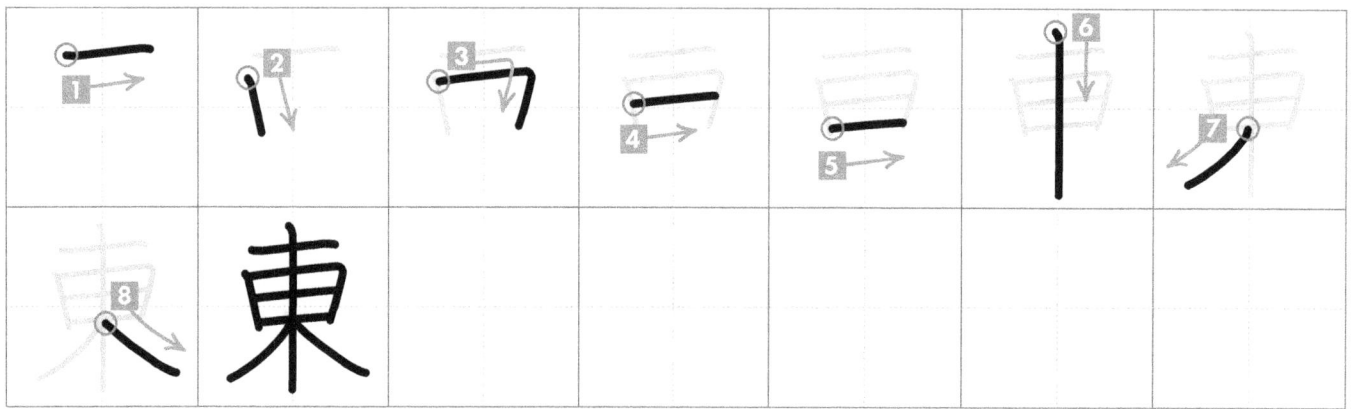

## PRACTICE
*Trace and practice this Kanji below*

STYLES  東 東 東 東 東 東 東 東

| KANJI # | RADICAL | STROKES | MEANING | | UNICODE |
|---|---|---|---|---|---|
| 0004 | 口 | 5 | four, 4 | | 56DB |

## 四

**ONYOMI**
シ
*shi*

**KUNYOMI**
よ(つ)、よん
*yo(tsu), yon*

**VOCABULARY**

四季 (しき) — four seasons
四月 (しがつ) — April
四十 (よんじゅう) — forty

十四 (じゅうよん) — fourteen
真四角 (ましかく) — square
長四角 (ながしかく) — rectangle

## STROKE ORDER

How this Kanji is drawn

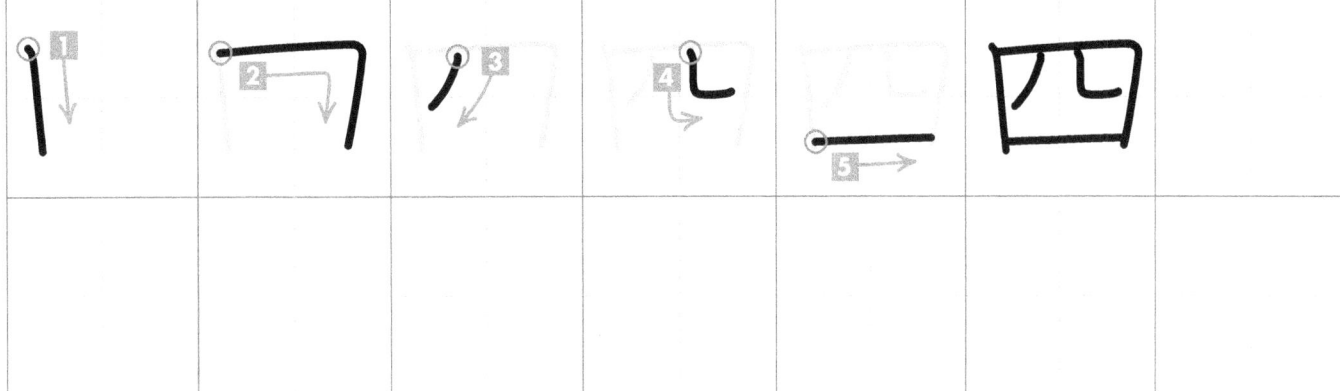

## PRACTICE

Trace and practice this Kanji below

STYLES 四 四 四 四 四 四 四 四

| KANJI # | RADICAL | STROKES | MEANING | UNICODE |
|---|---|---|---|---|
| 1711 | 人 | 4 | now, the present | 4ECA |

**ONYOMI**
コン、キン
*kon, kin*

**KUNYOMI**
いま
*ima*

**VOCABULARY**

今日 (きょう) — today; this day
今年 (ことし) — this year
今月 (こんげつ) — this month

今度 (こんど) — this time
今朝 (けさ) — this morning
今週 (こんしゅう) — this week

## STROKE ORDER

How this Kanji is drawn

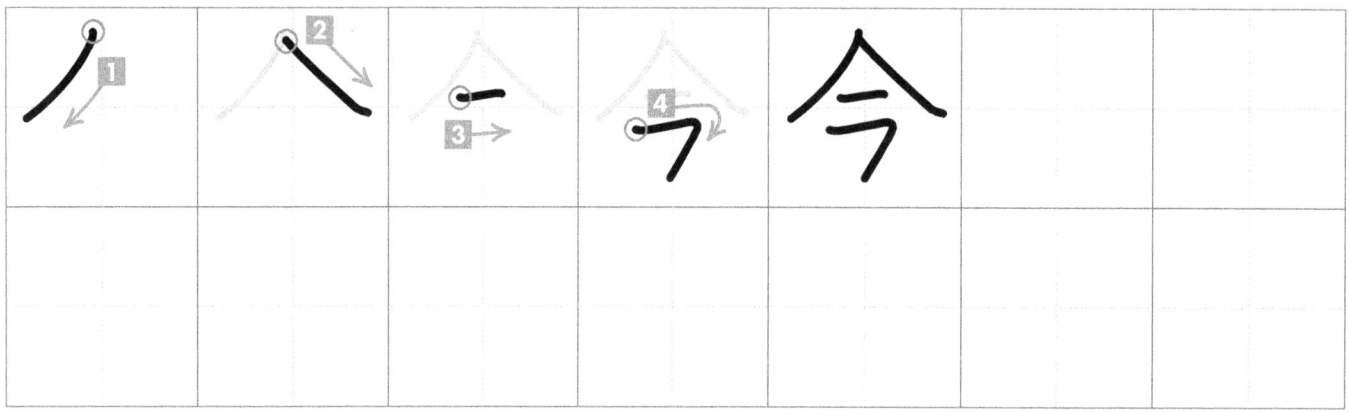

## PRACTICE

Trace and practice this Kanji below

**STYLES**

| KANJI # | RADICAL | STROKES | MEANING | | UNICODE |
|---|---|---|---|---|---|
| 0287 | 金 | 8 | gold | | 91D1 |

**ONYOMI**

キン、コン、ゴン
*kin, kon, gon*

**KUNYOMI**

かね、かな-、-がね
*kane, kana, gane*

**VOCABULARY**

金属 (きんぞく) — metal
金曜 (きんよう) — Friday
金銭 (きんせん) — money; cash

料金 (りょうきん) — fee; charge
借金 (しゃっきん) — debt, loan
資金 (しきん) — funds; capital

## STROKE ORDER

*How this Kanji is drawn*

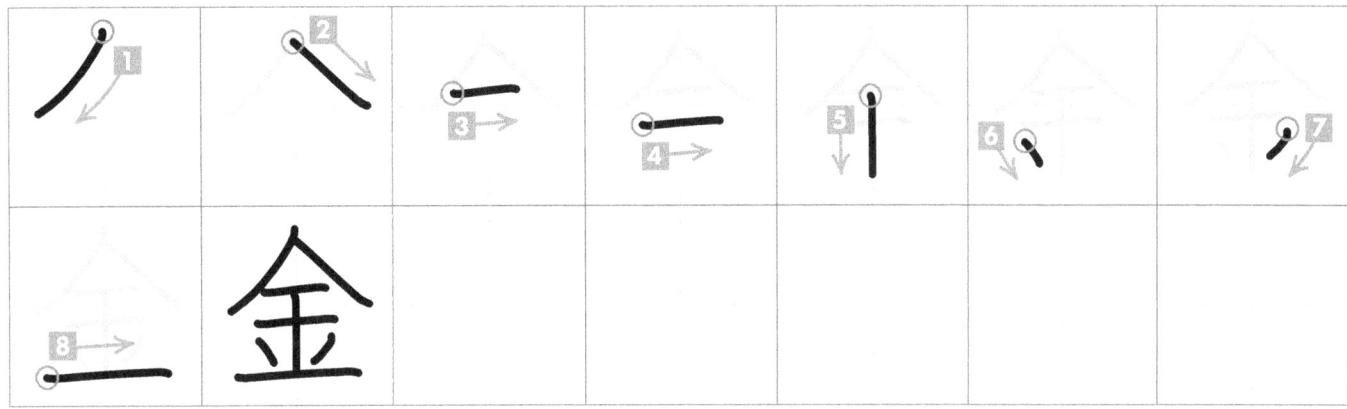

## PRACTICE

*Trace and practice this Kanji below*

## STYLES

53

| KANJI # | RADICAL | STROKES | MEANING | | UNICODE |
|---|---|---|---|---|---|
| 0009 | 丿 | 2 | nine, 9 | | 4E5D |

**ONYOMI**
キュウ、ク
*kyuu, ku*

**KUNYOMI**
ここの(つ)
*kokono(tsu)*

**VOCABULARY**

| | | | |
|---|---|---|---|
| 九月 (くがつ) | September | 二九 (にく) | twenty nine |
| 九時 (くじ) | nine o'clock | 八九分 (はっくぶ) | nearly; almost |
| 九分 (くぶ) | nine parts | 十九 (じゅうきゅう) | nineteen |

**STROKE ORDER** — How this Kanji is drawn

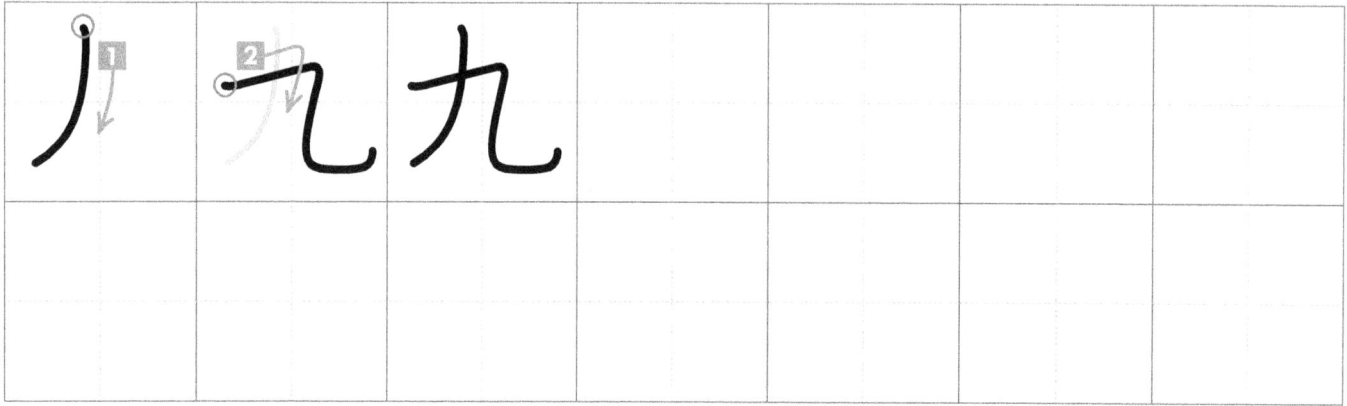

**PRACTICE** — Trace and practice this Kanji below

**STYLES** 九 九 九 九 九 九 九 九

| KANJI # | RADICAL | STROKES | MEANING | | UNICODE |
|---|---|---|---|---|---|
| 0842 | 入 | 2 | **enter, insert** | | 5165 |

## 入

**ONYOMI**

ニュウ
*nyuu*

**KUNYOMI**

い(る)、はい(る)
*i(ru), hai(ru)*

**VOCABULARY**

入る (はい) to enter; to go into
入場 (にゅうじょう) entrance; admission
入力 (にゅうりょく) input; (data) entry

収入 (しゅうにゅう) income; receipts
購入 (こうにゅう) purchase; buy
加入 (かにゅう) becoming a member

## STROKE ORDER

How this Kanji is drawn

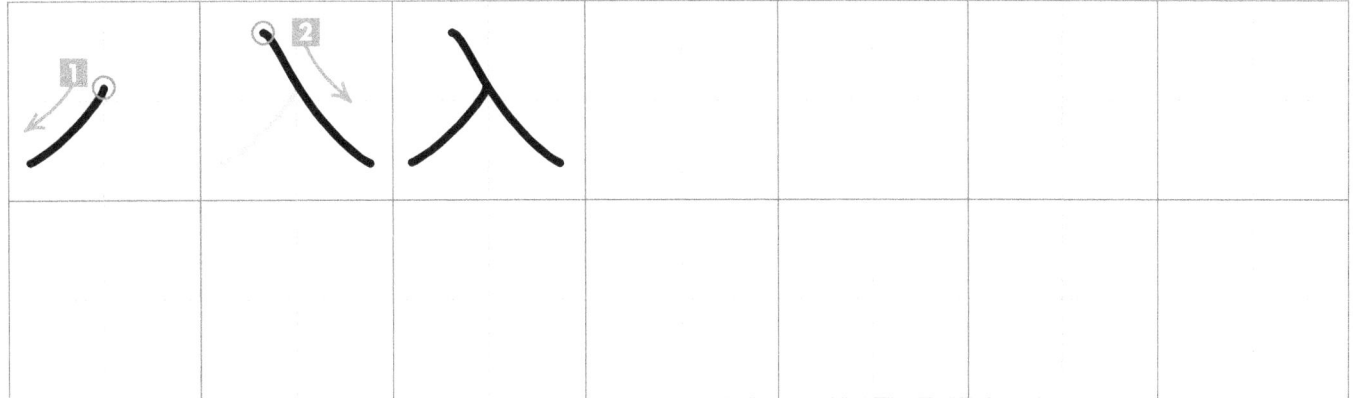

## PRACTICE

Trace and practice this Kanji below

STYLES

| KANJI # | RADICAL | STROKES | MEANING | | UNICODE |
|---|---|---|---|---|---|
| 0346 | 子 | 8 | study, learning, science | | 5B66 |

学

**ONYOMI**
ガク
*gaku*

**KUNYOMI**
まな(ぶ)
*mana(bu)*

**VOCABULARY**

学校 (がっこう) — school
学生 (がくせい) — student
学習 (がくしゅう) — study; learning

中学 (ちゅうがく) — middle school
科学 (かがく) — science
文学 (ぶんがく) — literature

## STROKE ORDER
*How this Kanji is drawn*

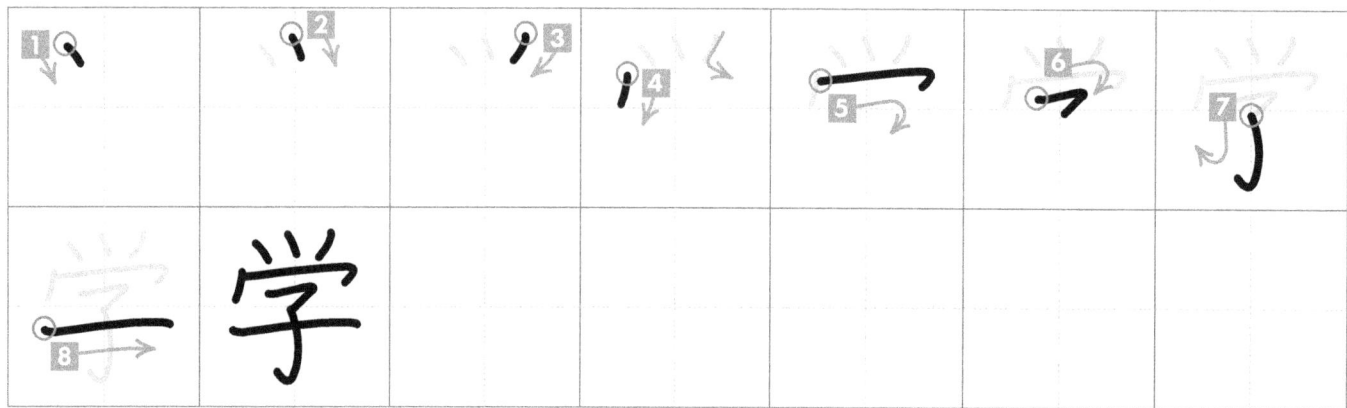

## PRACTICE
*Trace and practice this Kanji below*

**STYLES** 学 学 学 学 学 学 学 学

| KANJI # | RADICAL | STROKES | MEANING | UNICODE |
|---|---|---|---|---|
| 0329 | 高 | 10 | tall, high, expensive | 9AD8 |

### ONYOMI
コウ
*kou*

### KUNYOMI
たか(い)
*taka(i)*

### VOCABULARY

| | | | |
|---|---|---|---|
| 高い (たか) | high; tall | 最高 (さいこう) | highest; best |
| 高度 (こうど) | altitude; height | 標高 (ひょうこう) | elevation |
| 高速 (こうそく) | high speed; high gear | 小高い (こだか) | slightly elevated |

## STROKE ORDER
*How this Kanji is drawn*

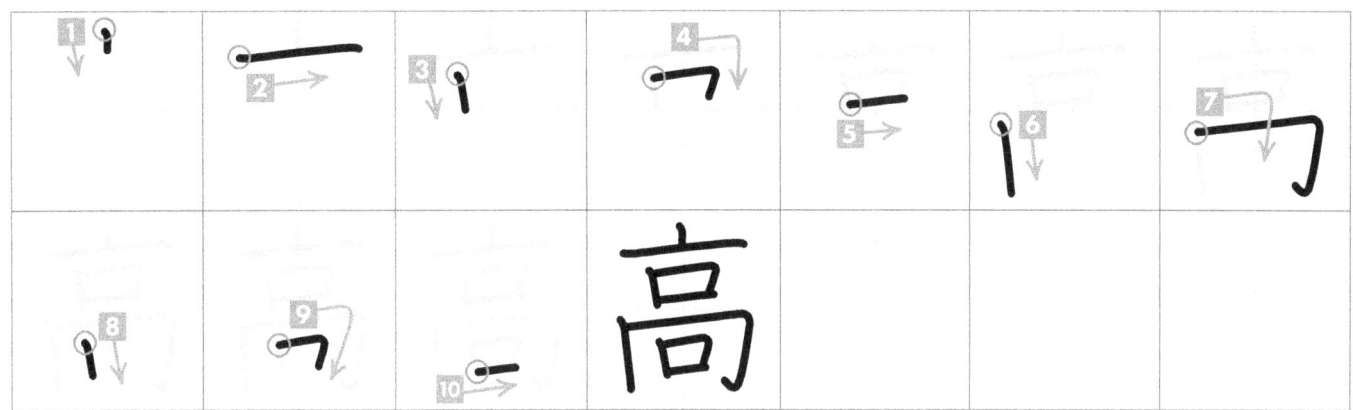

## PRACTICE
*Trace and practice this Kanji below*

## STYLES

高 髙 高 高 高 高 高 高

| KANJI # | RADICAL | STROKES | MEANING | UNICODE |
|---|---|---|---|---|
| 1952 | 冂 | 4 | circle, yen (Japanese monetary unit), round | 5186 |

## 円

**ONYOMI**
エン
*en*

**KUNYOMI**
まる(い)
*maru(i)*

**VOCABULARY**

| | | | | |
|---|---|---|---|---|
| 円い (まるい) | round; circular | 楕円 (だえん) | ellipse |
| 円滑 (えんかつ) | smooth; undisturbed | 半円 (はんえん) | semicircle |
| 円盤 (えんばん) | disk; discus; platter | 大円 (だいえん) | large circle |

### STROKE ORDER
*How this Kanji is drawn*

### PRACTICE
*Trace and practice this Kanji below*

### STYLES

| KANJI # | RADICAL | STROKES | MEANING | UNICODE |
|---|---|---|---|---|
| 0099 | 子 | 3 | child | 5B50 |

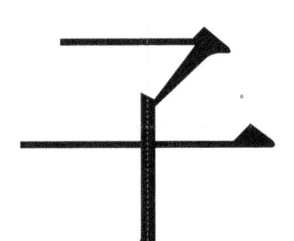

**ONYOMI**
シ、ス、ツ
*shi, su, tsu*

**KUNYOMI**
こ、-こ(ね)
*ko, ne*

**VOCABULARY**

| | | | |
|---|---|---|---|
| 子孫 (しそん) | descendants | 男子 (だんし) | youth; young man |
| 子女 (しじょ) | sons and daughters | 電子 (でんし) | electron |
| 子分 (こぶん) | henchman; follower | 女子 (じょし) | woman; girl |

## STROKE ORDER
*How this Kanji is drawn*

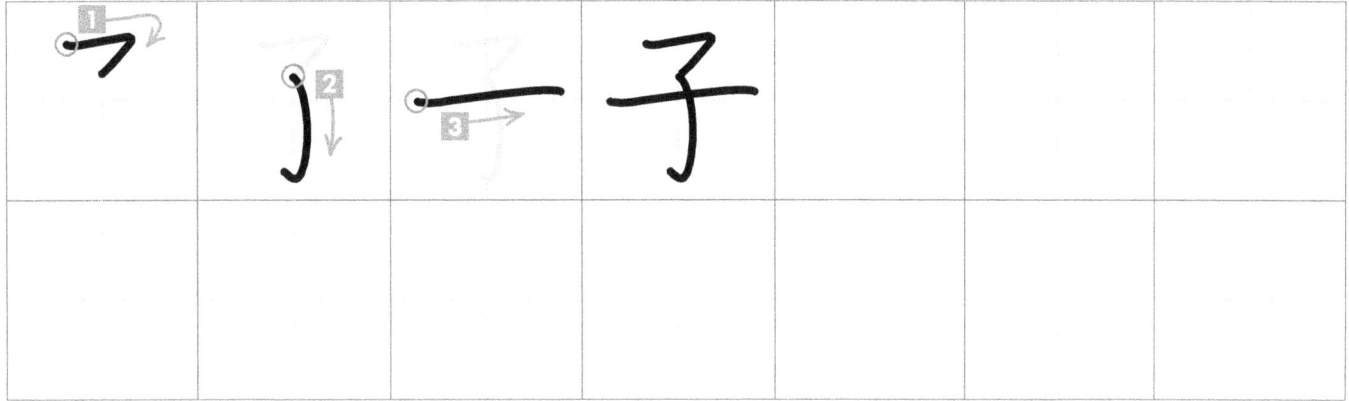

## PRACTICE
*Trace and practice this Kanji below*

**STYLES** 子 子 子 子 子 子 子 子

| KANJI # | RADICAL | STROKES | MEANING | UNICODE |
|---|---|---|---|---|
| 0116 | 夕 | 5 | outside | 5916 |

### ONYOMI
ガイ、ゲ
*gai, ge*

### KUNYOMI
そと、ほか、はず(す)、と-
*soto, hoka, hazu-, to-*

### VOCABULARY

| | | | |
|---|---|---|---|
| 外国 (がいこく) | foreign country | 海外 (かいがい) | foreign; abroad |
| 外部 (がいぶ) | the outside | 意外 (いがい) | unexpected |
| 外科 (げか) | surgery | 郊外 (こうがい) | suburb; outskirts |

## STROKE ORDER
How this Kanji is drawn

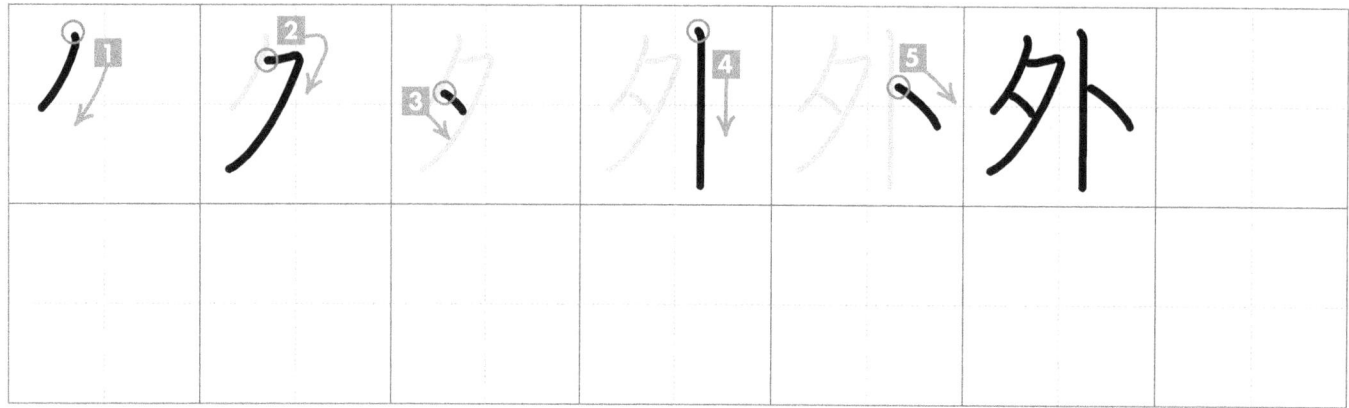

## PRACTICE
Trace and practice this Kanji below

STYLES

60

| KANJI # | RADICAL | STROKES | MEANING | UNICODE |
|---|---|---|---|---|
| 0008 | 八 | 2 | **eight, 8** | 516B |

## 八

**ONYOMI**

ハチ
*hachi*

**KUNYOMI**

や(つ)、よう
*ya(tsu), you*

**VOCABULARY**

| | | | | |
|---|---|---|---|---|
| 八十 (はちじゅう) | eighty | | 十八 (じゅうはち) | eighteen |
| 八月 (はちがつ) | August | | 二八 (にはち) | sixteen |
| 八時 (はちじ) | eight o'clock | | 百八 (ひゃくはち) | 108 |

### STROKE ORDER
*How this Kanji is drawn*

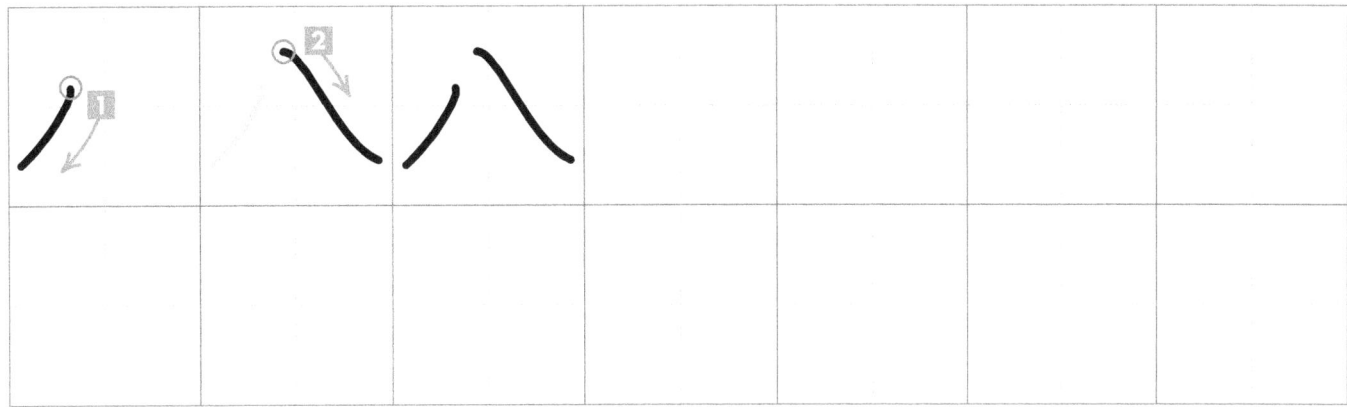

### PRACTICE
*Trace and practice this Kanji below*

### STYLES

| KANJI # | RADICAL | STROKES | MEANING | | UNICODE |
|---|---|---|---|---|---|
| 0006 | 八 | 4 | six, 6 | | 516D |

## 六

**ONYOMI**
ロク
*roku*

**KUNYOMI**
む(つ)、むい
*mu(tsu), mui*

**VOCABULARY**

| | | | | |
|---|---|---|---|---|
| 六月 (ろくがつ) | June | | 才六 (さいろく) | kid; brat |
| 六十 (ろくじゅう) | sixty | | 6歳 (ろくさい) | 6 year old |
| 六角 (ろっかく) | hexagon | | 甚六 (じんろく) | dunce |

### STROKE ORDER — How this Kanji is drawn

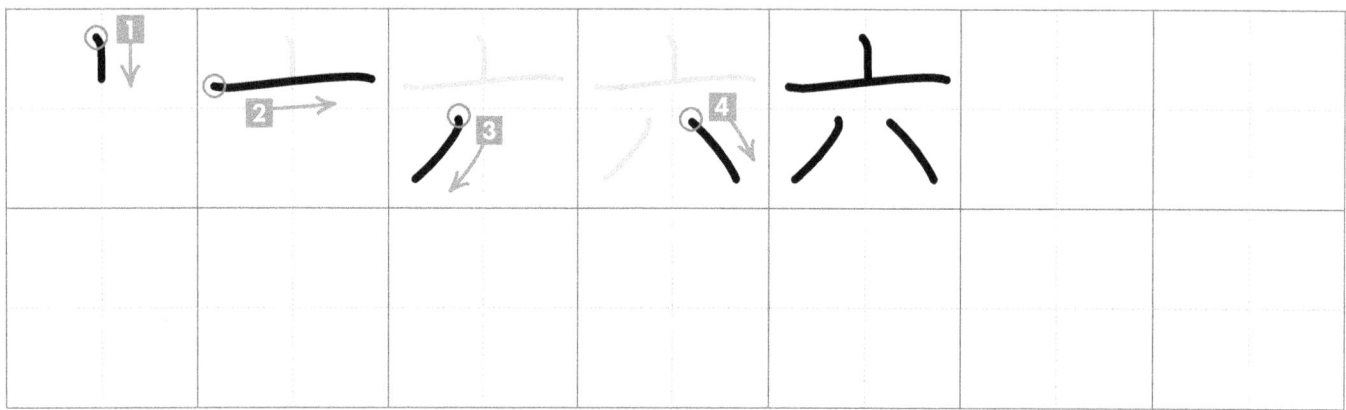

### PRACTICE — Trace and practice this Kanji below

**STYLES** 六 六 六 六 六 六 六 六

| KANJI # | RADICAL | STROKES | MEANING | UNICODE |
|---|---|---|---|---|
| 0051 | 口 | 3 | below, down, descend, give, low, inferior | 4E0B |

下

**ONYOMI**
カ、ゲ
*ka, ge*

**KUNYOMI**
した、しも、もと、さ(げる)、くだ(る)、お(ろす)
*shita, shimo, moto, sa(geru), kuda(ru), o(rosu)*

**VOCABULARY**

| | | | |
|---|---|---|---|
| 下手 (へた) | unskillful | 地下 (ちか) | basement |
| 下着 (したぎ) | underwear | 靴下 (くつした) | socks |
| 下る (くだ) | to descend | 低下 (ていか) | fall; decline |

## STROKE ORDER
*How this Kanji is drawn*

## PRACTICE
*Trace and practice this Kanji below*

## STYLES

下 下 下 下 下 下 下 下 下

63

| KANJI # | RADICAL | STROKES | MEANING | UNICODE |
|---|---|---|---|---|
| 2029 | 木 | 7 | come, due, next, cause, become | 6765 |

来

**ONYOMI**
ライ、タイ
*rai, tai*

**KUNYOMI**
く.る、きた.る、き、こ
*kuru, kitaru, ki, ko*

**VOCABULARY**

来年 (らいねん)    next year
来月 (らいげつ)    next month
来週 (らいしゅう)    next week

本来 (ほんらい)    originally
以来 (いらい)    since
外来 (がいらい)    foreign

**STROKE ORDER**      How this Kanji is drawn

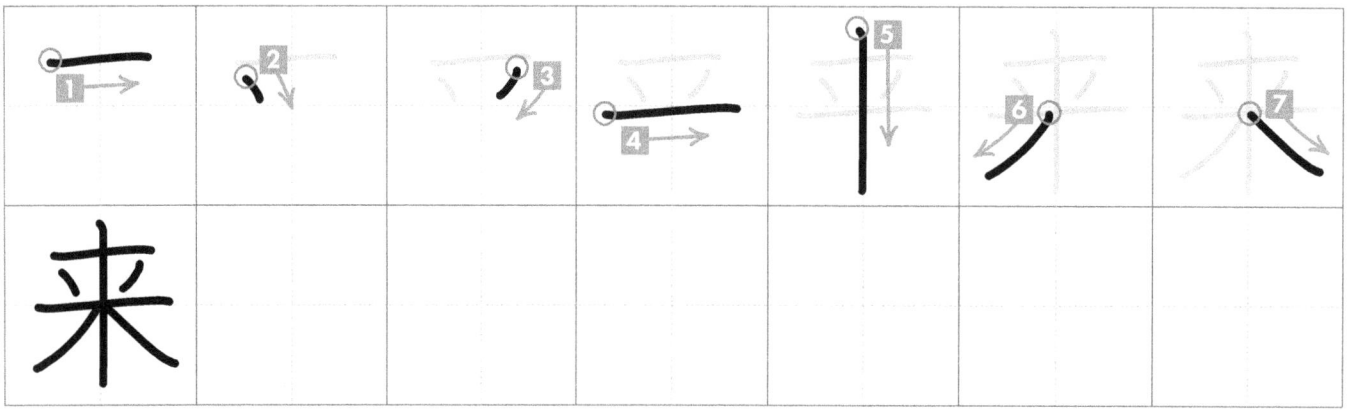

**PRACTICE**      Trace and practice this Kanji below

STYLES    来 来 来 来 来 来 来 来

| KANJI # | RADICAL | STROKES | MEANING | UNICODE |
|---|---|---|---|---|
| 2030 | 气 | 6 | spirit, mind, air, atmosphere, mood | 6C17 |

## 気

**ONYOMI**  
キ、ケ  
*ki, ke*

**KUNYOMI**  
いき  
*iki*

### VOCABULARY

| | | | |
|---|---|---|---|
| 気分 (きぶん) | feeling; mood | 電気 (でんき) | electricity |
| 気象 (きしょう) | weather; climate | 病気 (びょうき) | illness; disease |
| 気圧 (きあつ) | atmospheric pressure | 元気 (げんき) | lively |

### STROKE ORDER
*How this Kanji is drawn*

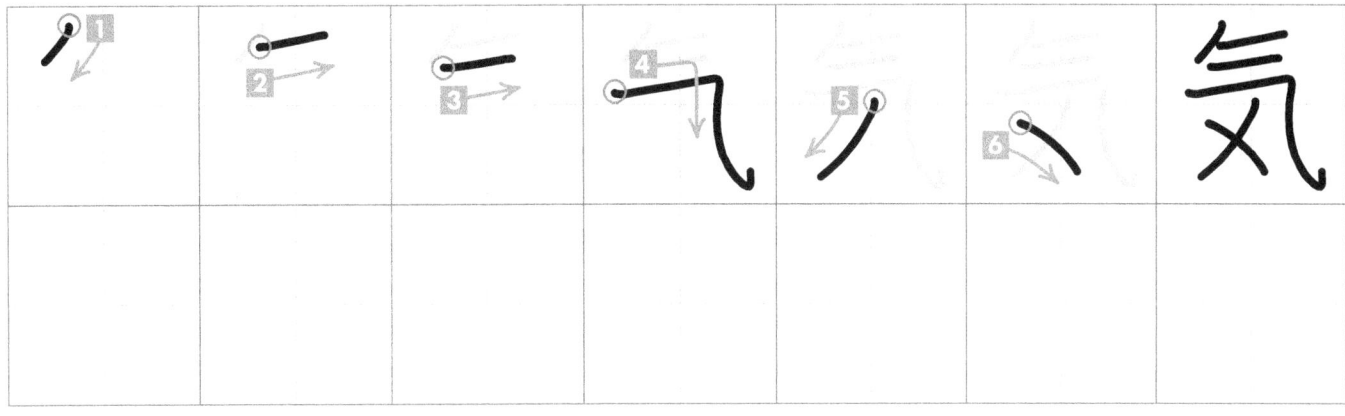

### PRACTICE
*Trace and practice this Kanji below*

### STYLES

気 気 気 気 気 気 気 気

65

| KANJI # | RADICAL | STROKES | MEANING | | UNICODE |
|---|---|---|---|---|---|
| 0110 | 小 | 3 | little, small | | 5C0F |

**ONYOMI**
ショウ
*shou*

**KUNYOMI**
ちい(さい)、
こ-、お-、さ-
*chii(sai), ko-, o-, sa-*

**VOCABULARY**

小供 (こども) — child; children
小説 (しょうせつ) — novel
小女 (しょうじょ) — little girl

大小 (だいしょう) — large and small
縮小 (しゅくしょう) — reduction
最小 (さいしょう) — smallest

## STROKE ORDER
How this Kanji is drawn

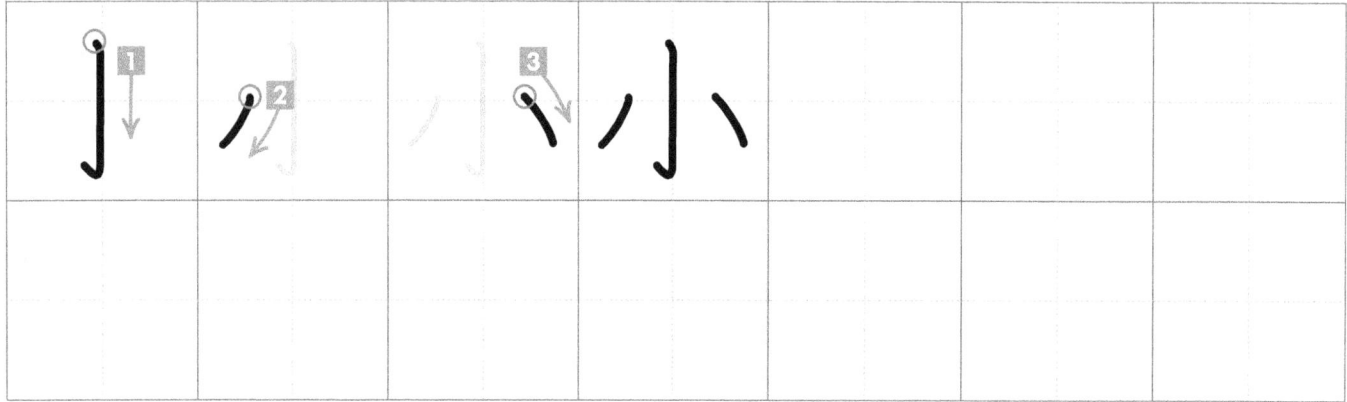

## PRACTICE
Trace and practice this Kanji below

## STYLES

| KANJI # | RADICAL | STROKES | MEANING | UNICODE |
|---------|---------|---------|---------|---------|
| 0007 | 一 | 2 | **seven, 7** | 4E03 |

## 七

**ONYOMI**
シチ
*shichi*

**KUNYOMI**
なな(つ)、なの
*nana(tsu), nano*

**VOCABULARY**

| | | | |
|---|---|---|---|
| 七月 (しちがつ) | July | 十七 (じゅうしち) | seventeen |
| 七十 (ななじゅう) | seventy | 五七 (ごしち) | five and seven |
| 七分 (しちぶん) | seven minutes | 七星 (しちせい) | the Big Dipper |

## STROKE ORDER
*How this Kanji is drawn*

## PRACTICE
*Trace and practice this Kanji below*

## STYLES
七 七 七 七 七 七 七 七

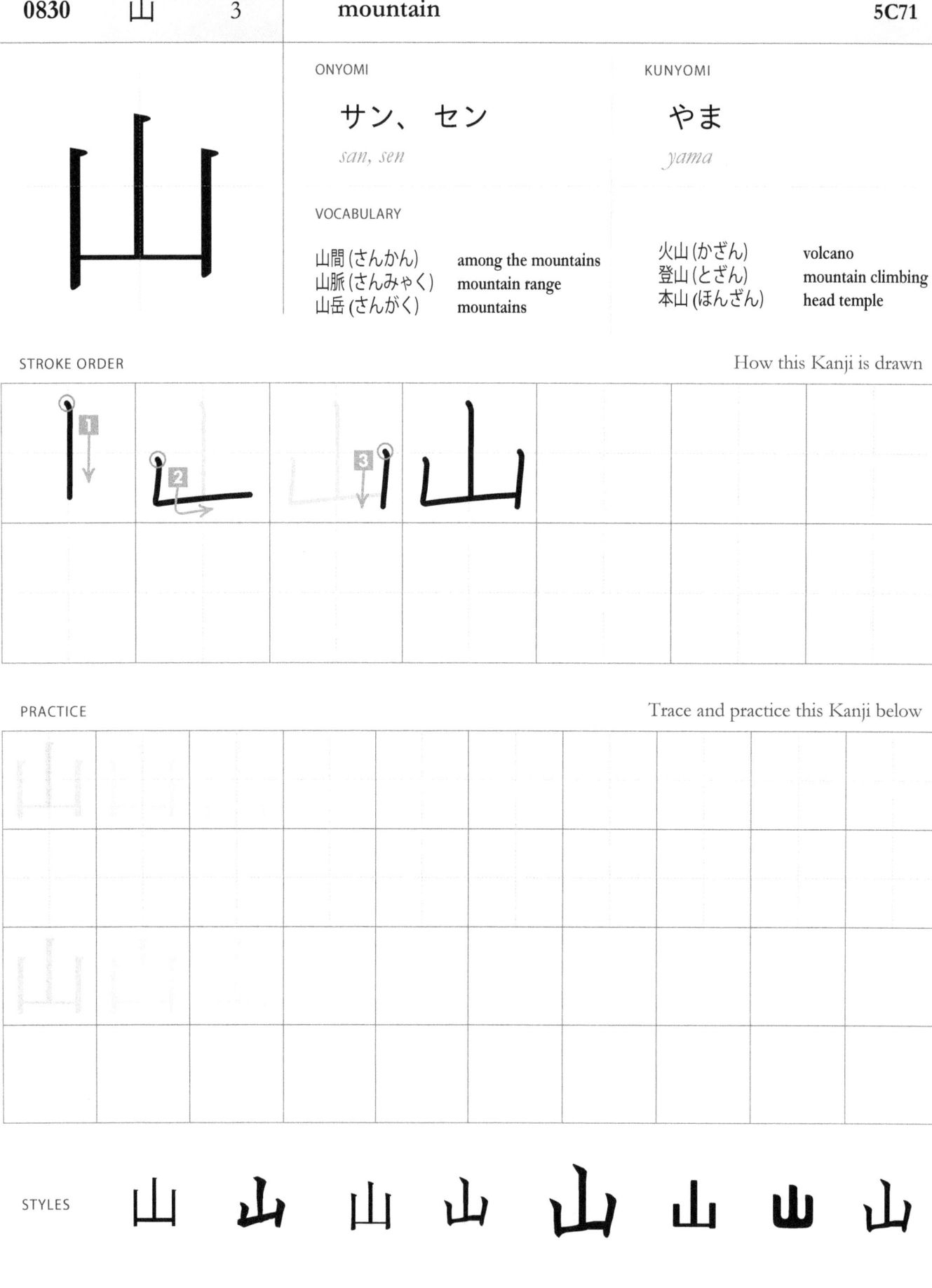

| KANJI # | RADICAL | STROKES | MEANING | UNICODE |
|---|---|---|---|---|
| 0368 | 言 | 13 | tale, talk | 8A71 |

話

**ONYOMI**
ワ
*wa*

**KUNYOMI**
はな(す)、はなし
*hana(su), hanashi*

**VOCABULARY**

話題 (わだい) topic; subject
話中 (はなしちゅう) busy (phone)
話々 (はなしばなし) small talk

会話 (かいわ) conversation
世話 (せわ) looking after
神話 (しんわ) myth; legend

## STROKE ORDER
*How this Kanji is drawn*

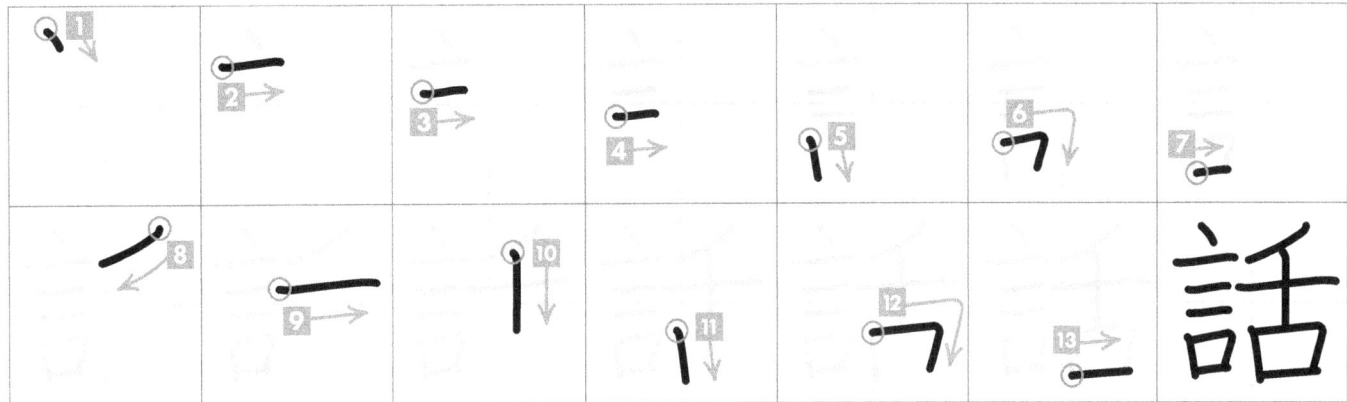

## PRACTICE
*Trace and practice this Kanji below*

STYLES: 話 話 話 話 話 話 話 話

| KANJI # | RADICAL | STROKES | MEANING | UNICODE |
|---|---|---|---|---|
| 0102 | 女 | 3 | woman, female | 5973 |

女

**ONYOMI**

ジョ
*jo*

**KUNYOMI**

おんな、め
*onnna, me*

**VOCABULARY**

| 女神 (めがみ) | goddess | 彼女 (かのじょ) | she; her |
| 女子 (じょし) | woman; girl | 男女 (だんじょ) | men and women |
| 女優 (じょゆう) | actress | 王女 (おうじょ) | princess |

**STROKE ORDER** — How this Kanji is drawn

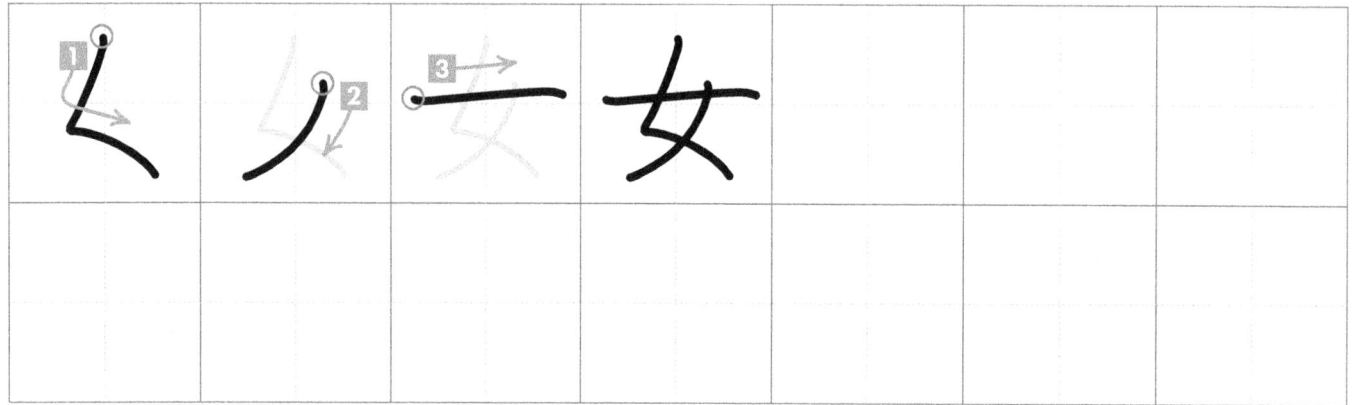

**PRACTICE** — Trace and practice this Kanji below

**STYLES**   女 女 女 女 女 女 女 女

| KANJI # | RADICAL | STROKES | MEANING | UNICODE |
|---|---|---|---|---|
| 0480 | 匕 | 5 | **north** | 5317 |

### ONYOMI
ホク
*hoku*

### KUNYOMI
きた
*kita*

### VOCABULARY

| | | | | |
|---|---|---|---|---|
| 北東 (ほくとう) | northeast | | 敗北 (はいぼく) | defeat |
| 北西 (ほくせい) | northwest | | 台北 (タイペイ) | Taipei |
| 北極 (ほっきょく) | North Pole | | 以北 (いほく) | north of |

## STROKE ORDER
*How this Kanji is drawn*

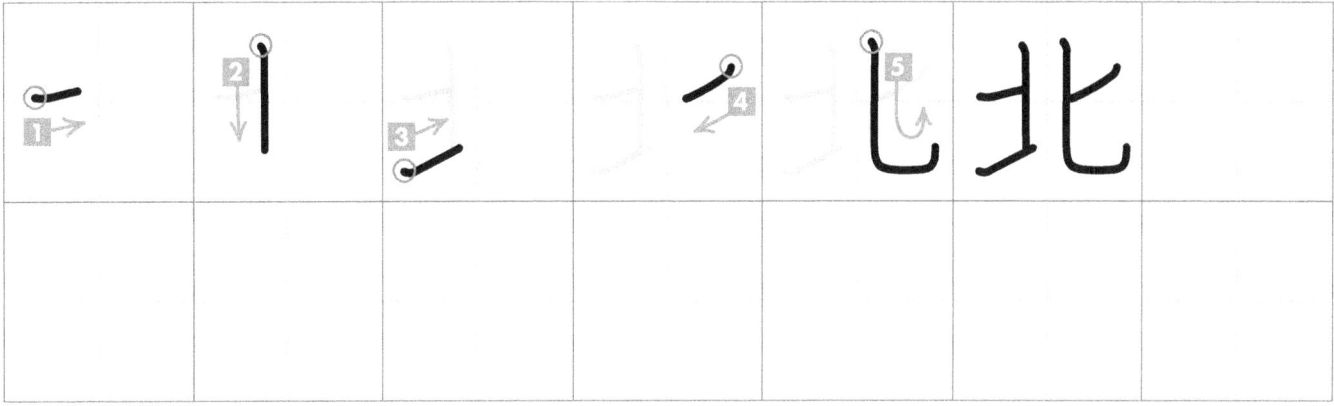

## PRACTICE
*Trace and practice this Kanji below*

## STYLES

北 北 北 北 北 北 北 北

71

| KANJI # | RADICAL | STROKES | MEANING | UNICODE |
|---|---|---|---|---|
| 0610 | 十 | 4 | **noon, sign of the horse** | 5348 |

**ONYOMI**
ゴ
*go*

**KUNYOMI**
うま
*uma*

**VOCABULARY**

午後 (ごご) afternoon
午前 (ごぜん) morning
午飯 (ごはん) lunch

亭午 (ていご) noon
子午環 (しごかん) meridian circle
午睡 (ごすい) nap

## STROKE ORDER

How this Kanji is drawn

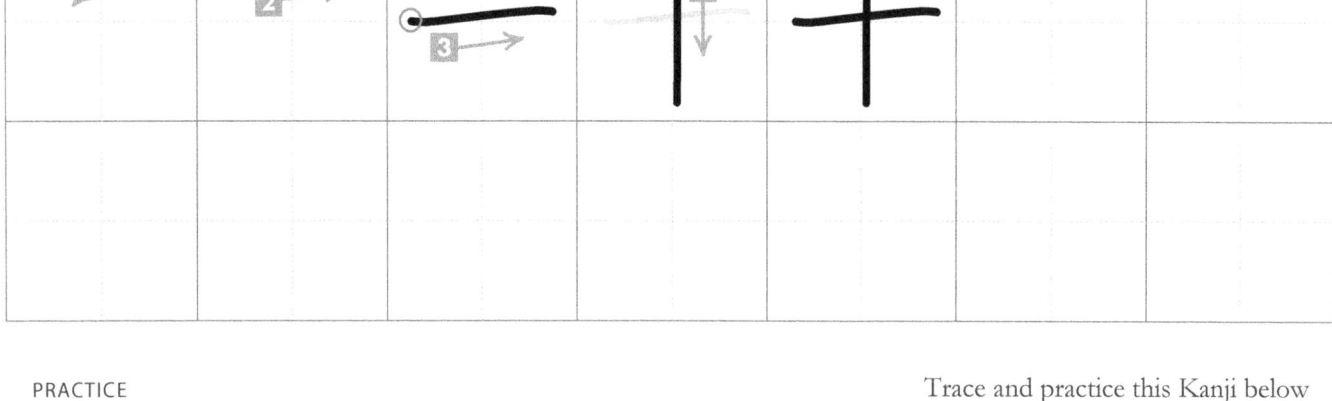

## PRACTICE

Trace and practice this Kanji below

**STYLES** 午 午 午 午 午 午 午 午

72

| KANJI # | RADICAL | STROKES | MEANING | UNICODE |
|---|---|---|---|---|
| 0038 | 白 | 6 | hundred | 767E |

**ONYOMI**

ヒャク、ビャク
*hyaku, byaku*

**KUNYOMI**

もも
*momo*

**VOCABULARY**

百万 (ひゃくまん) one million
百姓 (ひゃくしょう) farmer; peasant
百年 (ひゃくねん) century

何百 (なんびゃく) hundreds
二百 (にひゃく) two hundred
四百 (よんひゃく) four hundred

**STROKE ORDER** — How this Kanji is drawn

**PRACTICE** — Trace and practice this Kanji below

**STYLES**

| KANJI # | RADICAL | STROKES | MEANING | UNICODE |
|---|---|---|---|---|
| 0349 | 曰 | 10 | write | 66F8 |

## ONYOMI
ショ
*sho*

## KUNYOMI
か(く)
*kaku*

## VOCABULARY

書類 (しょるい) — documents
書店 (しょてん) — bookshop; bookstore
書物 (しょもつ) — books

読書 (どくしょ) — reading
辞書 (じしょ) — dictionary
白書 (はくしょ) — white paper

## STROKE ORDER
*How this Kanji is drawn*

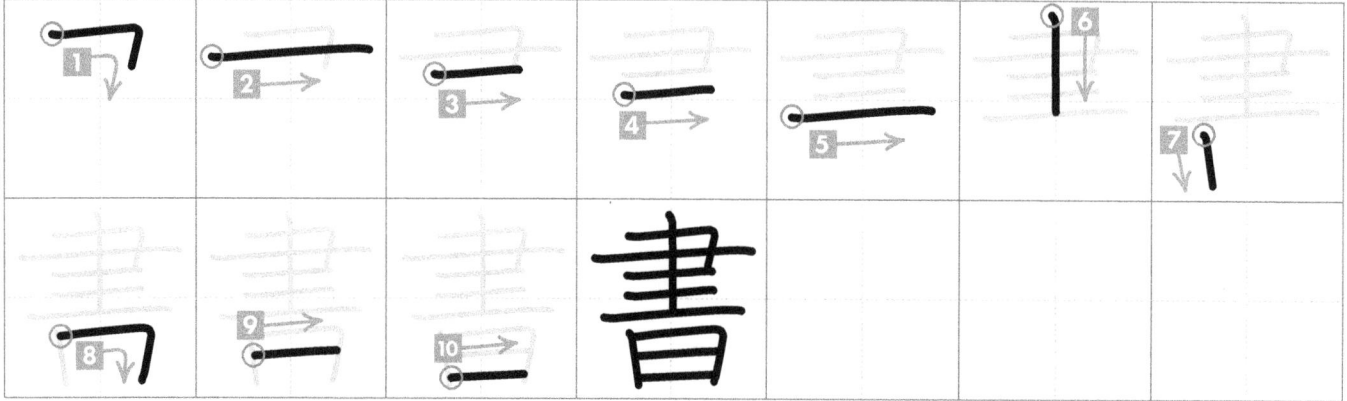

## PRACTICE
*Trace and practice this Kanji below*

## STYLES
書 書 書 書 書 書 書 書

| KANJI # | RADICAL | STROKES | MEANING | UNICODE |
|---|---|---|---|---|
| 0263 | 儿 | 6 | before, ahead, previous, future, precedence | 5148 |

先

**ONYOMI**
セン
*sen*

**KUNYOMI**
さき、ま(ず)
*saki, ma(zu)*

**VOCABULARY**

| | | | |
|---|---|---|---|
| 先生 (せんせい) | teacher; master | 出先 (でさき) | one's destination |
| 先月 (せんげつ) | last month | 目先 (めさき) | near future |
| 先祖 (せんぞ) | ancestor | | |

## STROKE ORDER
*How this Kanji is drawn*

## PRACTICE
*Trace and practice this Kanji below*

## STYLES

先 先 先 先 先 先 先 先

75

| KANJI # | RADICAL | STROKES | MEANING | UNICODE |
|---|---|---|---|---|
| 0117 | 口 | 6 | name, noted, distinguished, reputation | 540D |

**ONYOMI**: メイ、ミョウ — *mei, myou*

**KUNYOMI**: な — *na*

## VOCABULARY

- 名人 (めいじん) — master; expert
- 名字 (みょうじ) — surname
- 名作 (めいさく) — masterpiece
- 有名 (ゆうめい) — famous
- 本名 (ほんみょう) — real name
- 題名 (だいめい) — title

## STROKE ORDER
*How this Kanji is drawn*

## PRACTICE
*Trace and practice this Kanji below*

## STYLES

| KANJI # | RADICAL | STROKES | MEANING | | UNICODE |
|---|---|---|---|---|---|
| 0134 | 巛 | 3 | river, stream | | 5DDD |

川

**ONYOMI**
セン
*sen*

**KUNYOMI**
かわ
*kawa*

**VOCABULARY**

川口 (かわぐち) — mouth of river
川端 (かわばた) — riverbank
川下 (かわしも) — downstream

河川 (かせん) — rivers
谷川 (たにがわ) — mountain stream
大川 (おおかわ) — big river

## STROKE ORDER
*How this Kanji is drawn*

## PRACTICE
*Trace and practice this Kanji below*

## STYLES

| KANJI # | RADICAL | STROKES | MEANING | | | UNICODE |
|---|---|---|---|---|---|---|
| 0040 | 十 | 3 | **thousand** | | | 5343 |

**ONYOMI**  
セン  
*sen*

**KUNYOMI**  
ち  
*chi*

**VOCABULARY**

| | | | |
|---|---|---|---|
| 千代 (せんだい) | thousand years | 三千 (さんぜん) | three thousand |
| 千生 (せんなり) | great collection | 何千 (なんぜん) | many thousand |
| 千万 (せんばん) | exceedingly | 四千 (よんせん) | four thousand |

**STROKE ORDER** — How this Kanji is drawn

**PRACTICE** — Trace and practice this Kanji below

**STYLES**

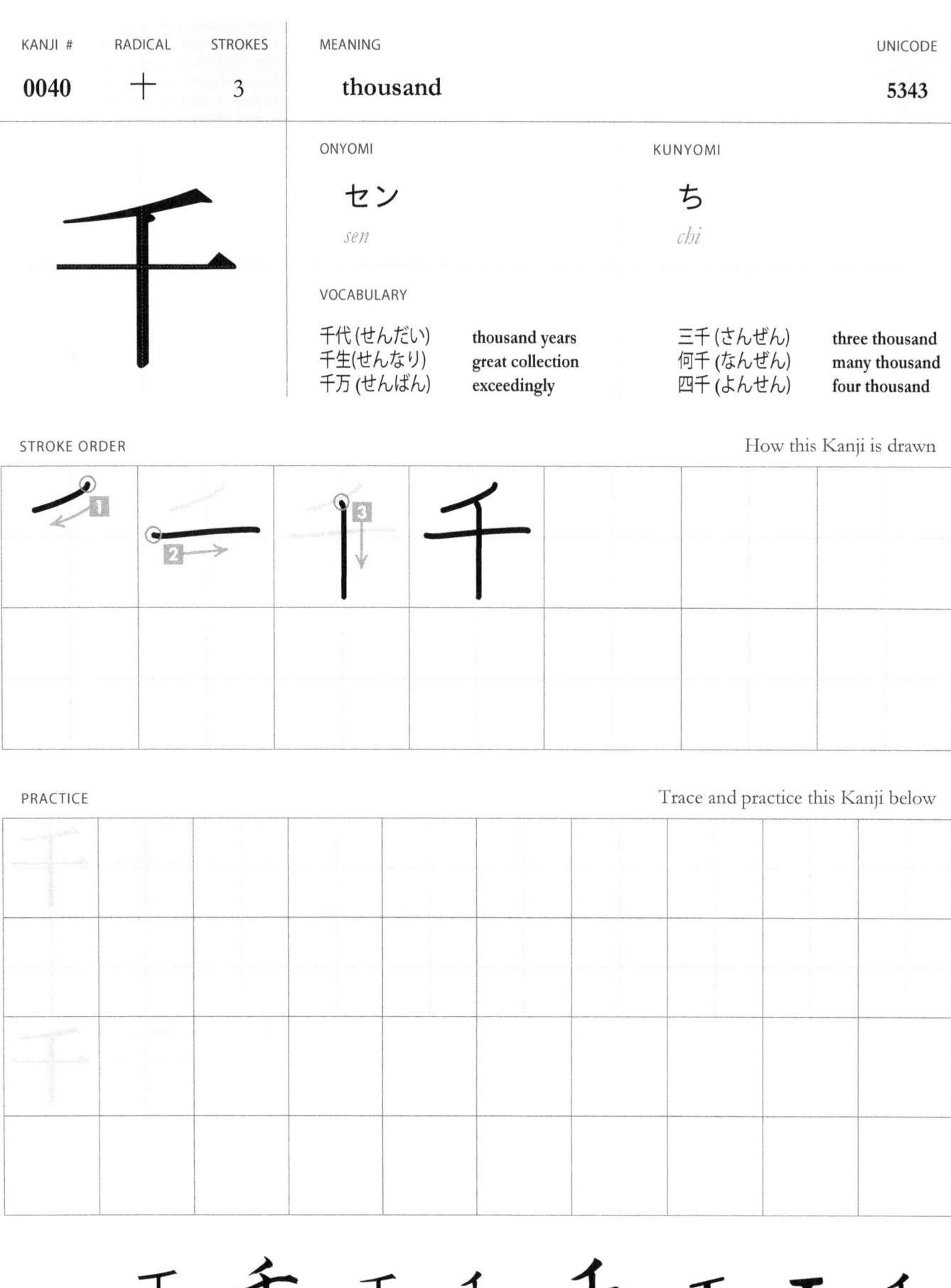

78

| KANJI # | RADICAL | STROKES | MEANING | UNICODE |
|---|---|---|---|---|
| 0137 | 水 | 4 | water | 6C34 |

水

**ONYOMI**
スイ
*sui*

**KUNYOMI**
みず
*mizu*

**VOCABULARY**

水道 (すいどう)　water supply
水泳 (すいえい)　swimming
水中 (すいちゅう)　underwater

下水 (げすい)　drainage
洪水 (こうずい)　flood
海水 (かいすい)　ocean water

## STROKE ORDER
How this Kanji is drawn

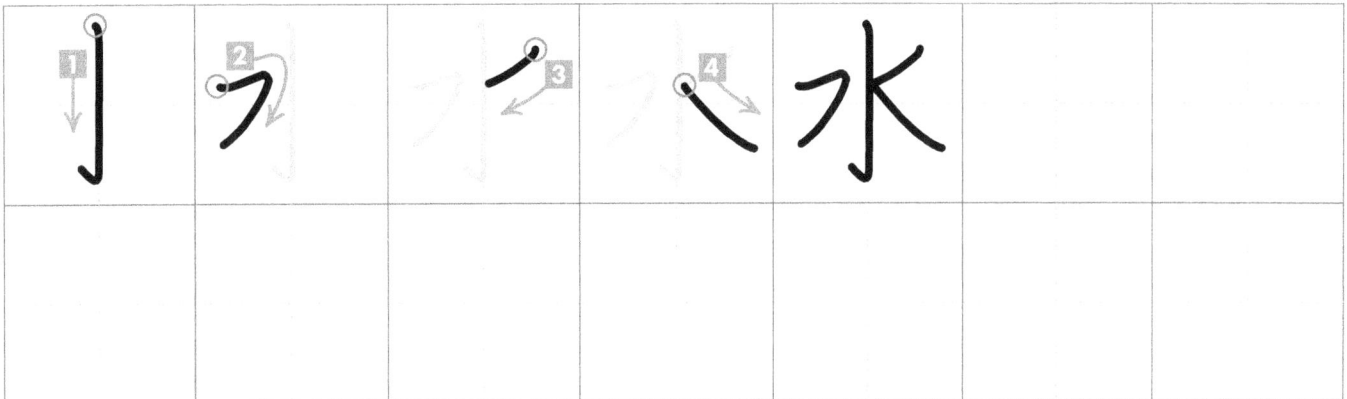

## PRACTICE
Trace and practice this Kanji below

STYLES　水　水　水　水　水　水　水　水

| KANJI # | RADICAL | STROKES | MEANING | UNICODE |
|---|---|---|---|---|
| 1286 | 十 | 5 | half, middle, odd number, semi- | 534A |

### ONYOMI
ハン
*han*

### KUNYOMI
なか(ば)
*naka(ba)*

### VOCABULARY

| | | | | |
|---|---|---|---|---|
| 半年 (はんとし) | half year | 大半 (たいはん) | majority |
| 半島 (はんとう) | peninsula | 後半 (こうはん) | second half |
| 半径 (はんけい) | radius | 前半 (ぜんはん) | first half |

## STROKE ORDER
How this Kanji is drawn

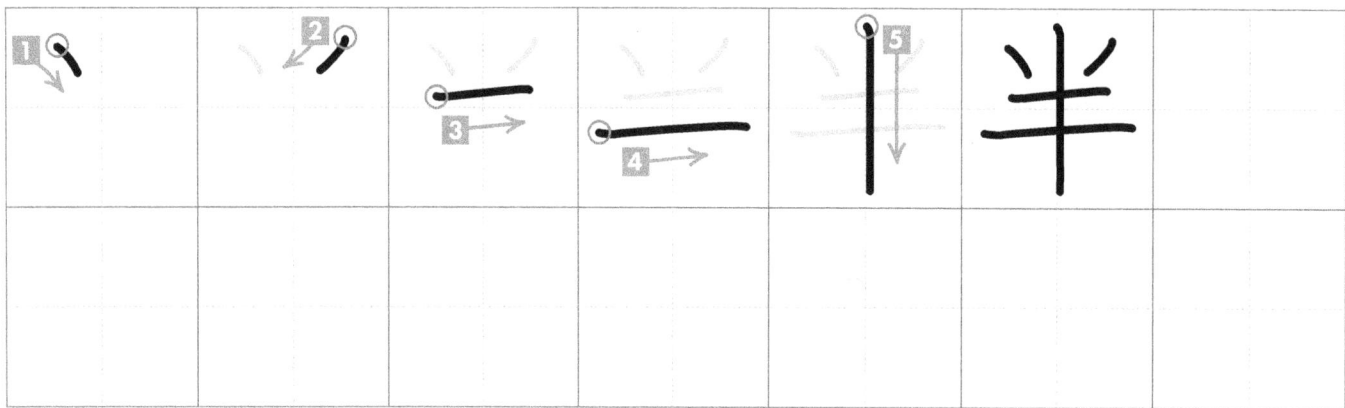

## PRACTICE
Trace and practice this Kanji below

STYLES  半 半 半 半 半 半 半 半

80

| KANJI # | RADICAL | STROKES | MEANING | UNICODE |
|---|---|---|---|---|
| 0923 | 田 | 7 | **male, man** | 7537 |

男

**ONYOMI**
ダン、ナン
*dan, nan*

**KUNYOMI**
おとこ、お
*otoko, o*

**VOCABULARY**

| | | | | |
|---|---|---|---|---|
| 男子 (だんし) | youth; young man | | 長男 (ちょうなん) | eldest son |
| 男前 (おとこまえ) | handsom man | | 三男 (さんなん) | three sons |
| 男優 (だんゆう) | actor | | 次男 (じなん) | second son |

**STROKE ORDER** — How this Kanji is drawn

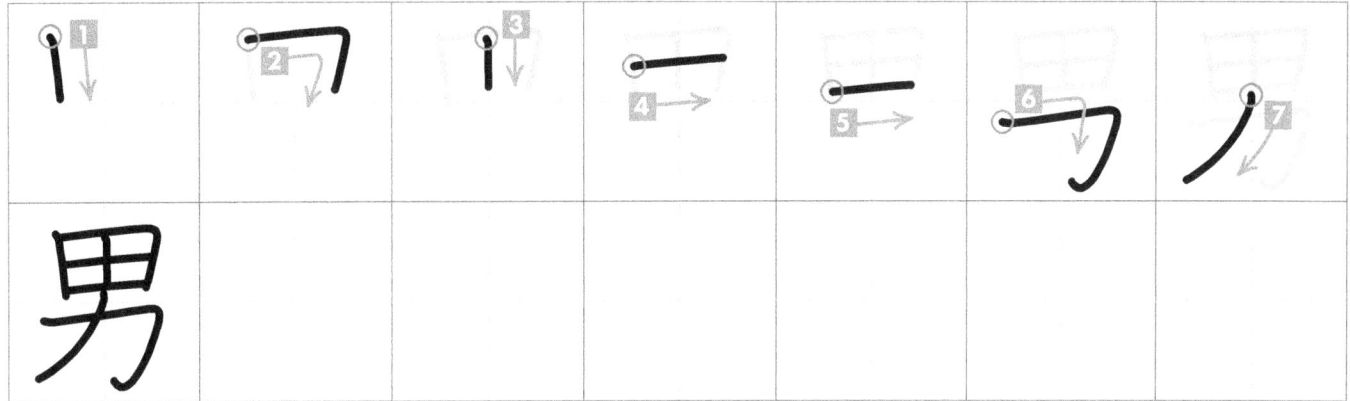

**PRACTICE** — Trace and practice this Kanji below

**STYLES**  男 男 男 男 男 男 男 男

| KANJI # | RADICAL | STROKES | MEANING | UNICODE |
|---|---|---|---|---|
| 1728 | 西 | 6 | **west** | 897F |

**ONYOMI**
セイ、サイ
*sei, sai*

**KUNYOMI**
にし
*nishi*

**VOCABULARY**

| | | | | |
|---|---|---|---|---|
| 西南 (せいなん) | south-west | 東西 (とうざい) | east and west |
| 西口 (にしぐち) | west entrance | 北西 (ほくせい) | northwest |
| 西北 (せいほく) | north-west | 南西 (なんせい) | southwest |

## STROKE ORDER
*How this Kanji is drawn*

## PRACTICE
*Trace and practice this Kanji below*

**STYLES**  西 西 西 西 西 西 西 西

| KANJI # | RADICAL | STROKES | MEANING | UNICODE |
|---|---|---|---|---|
| 0574 | 雨 | 13 | electricity, electric powered | 96FB |

# 電

### ONYOMI

デン

*den*

### VOCABULARY

電車 (でんしゃ) electric train
電話 (でんわ) telephone call
電力 (でんりょく) electric power

終電 (しゅうでん) last train
外電 (がいでん) foreign telegram
送電 (そうでん) electric supply

## STROKE ORDER

How this Kanji is drawn

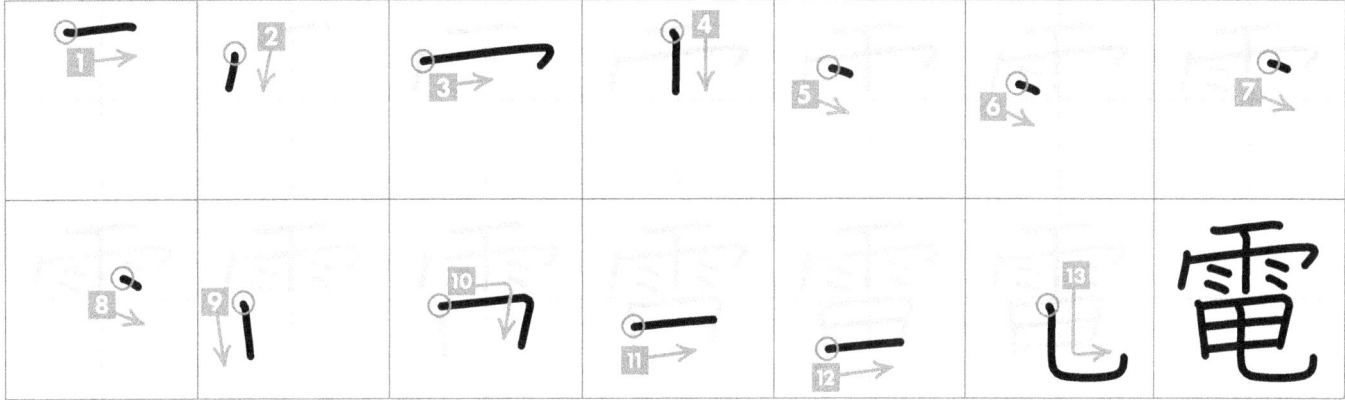

## PRACTICE

Trace and practice this Kanji below

STYLES 電 電 電 電 電 電 電 電

| KANJI # | RADICAL | STROKES | MEANING | UNICODE |
|---|---|---|---|---|
| 1371 | 木 | 10 | school | 6821 |

## 校

### ONYOMI
コウ
*kou*

### VOCABULARY

校長 (こうちょう) — principal
校舎 (こうしゃ) — school building
校庭 (こうてい) — schoolyard

母校 (ぼこう) — alma mater
登校 (とうこう) — going to school
分校 (ぶんこう) — branch school

## STROKE ORDER — How this Kanji is drawn

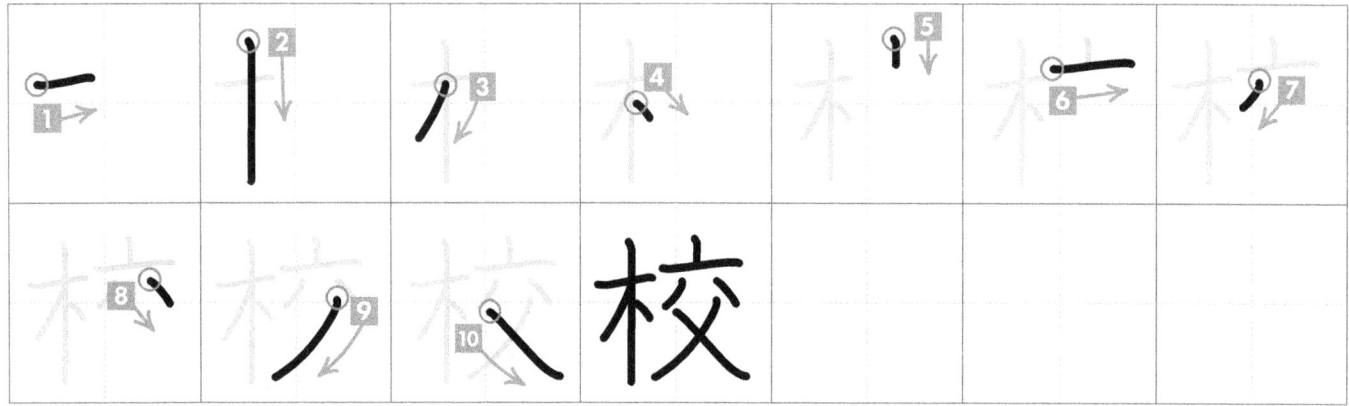

## PRACTICE — Trace and practice this Kanji below

STYLES 校 校 校 校 校 校 校 校

| KANJI # | RADICAL | STROKES | MEANING | UNICODE |
|---|---|---|---|---|
| 0371 | 言 | 14 | word, speech, language | 8A9E |

## 語

**ONYOMI**
ゴ
*go*

**KUNYOMI**
かた(る)
*kata(ru)*

**VOCABULARY**

| | | | |
|---|---|---|---|
| 語学 (ごがく) | language study | 用語 (ようご) | term; terminology |
| 語句 (ごく) | words; phrases | 物語 (ものがたり) | tale; story |
| 語気 (ごき) | manner of speaking | 国語 (こくご) | national language |

### STROKE ORDER
*How this Kanji is drawn*

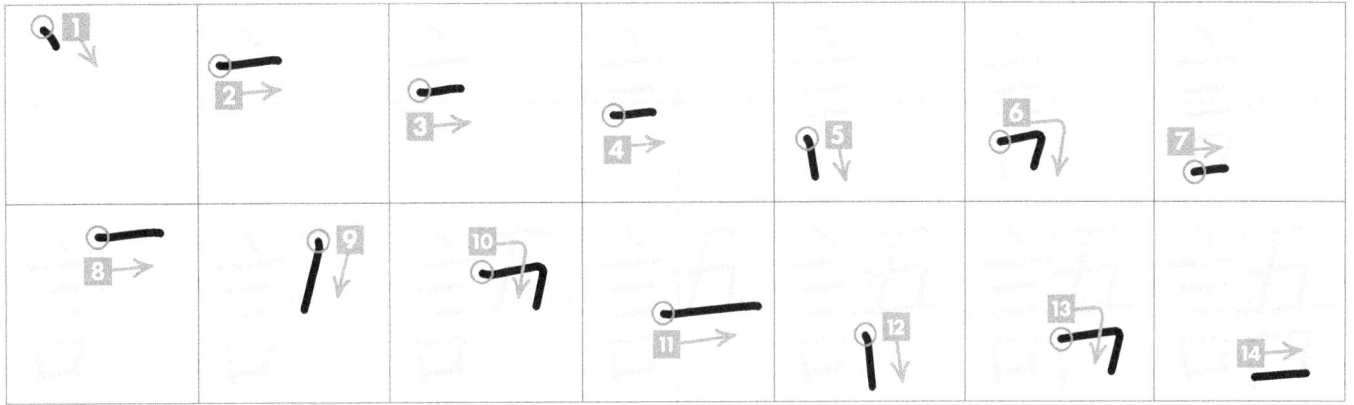

### PRACTICE
*Trace and practice this Kanji below*

### STYLES
語 語 語 語 語 語 語 語

85

| KANJI # | RADICAL | STROKES | MEANING | UNICODE |
|---|---|---|---|---|
| 0161 | 土 | 3 | soil, earth, ground | 571F |

**ONYOMI**

ド、ト
*do, to*

**KUNYOMI**

つち
*tsuchi*

**VOCABULARY**

| | | | |
|---|---|---|---|
| 土地 (とち) | plot of land | 国土 (こくど) | country; territory |
| 土圭 (とけい) | watch; clock | 領土 (りょうど) | dominion |
| 土曜 (どよう) | Saturday | 本土 (ほんど) | mainland |

## STROKE ORDER — How this Kanji is drawn

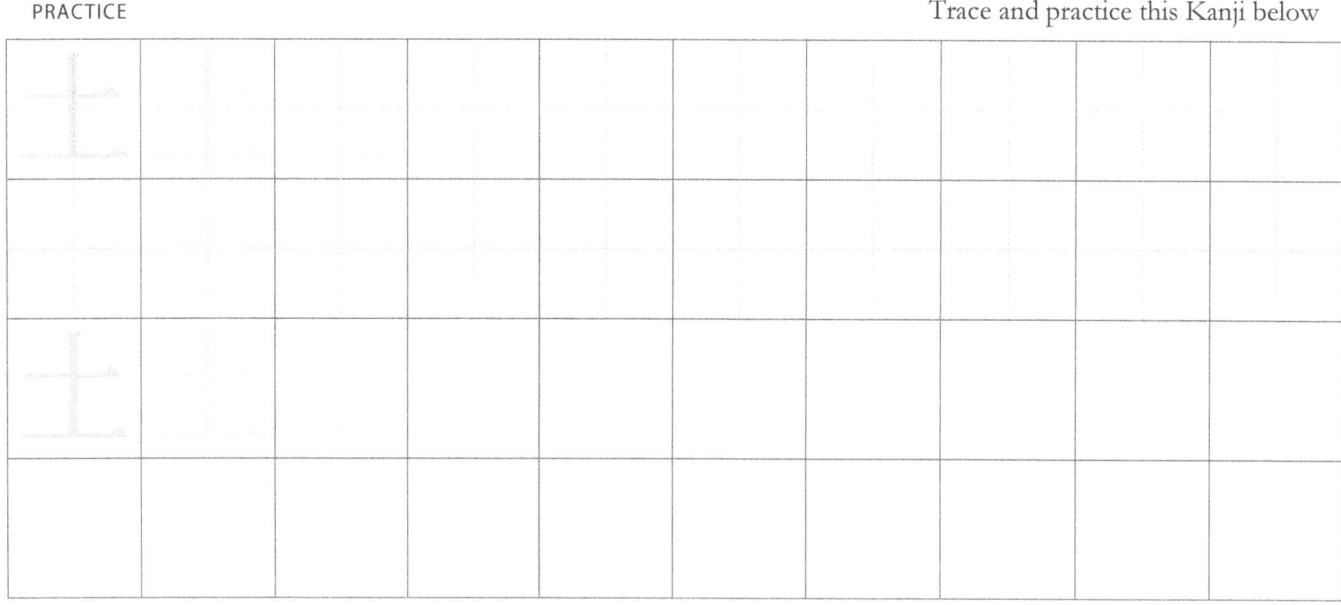

## PRACTICE — Trace and practice this Kanji below

## STYLES

土 土 土 土 土 土 土 土

86

| KANJI # | RADICAL | STROKES | MEANING | UNICODE |
|---|---|---|---|---|
| 0207 | 木 | 4 | tree, wood | 6728 |

**ONYOMI**

ボク、モク
*boku, moku*

**KUNYOMI**

き、こ-
*ki, ko*

**VOCABULARY**

| | | | |
|---|---|---|---|
| 木曜 (もくよう) | Thursday | 土木 (どぼく) | engineering works |
| 木材 (もくざい) | lumber; timber | 大木 (たいぼく) | large tree |
| 木立 (こだち) | grove of trees | 並木 (なみき) | roadside tree |

## STROKE ORDER

*How this Kanji is drawn*

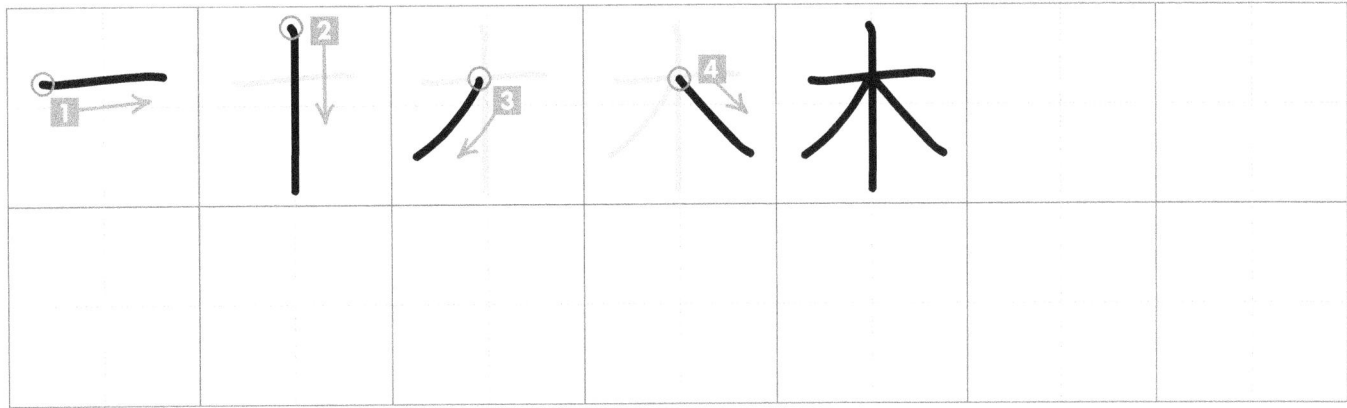

## PRACTICE

*Trace and practice this Kanji below*

## STYLES

木　木　木　木　木　木　木　木

87

| KANJI # | RADICAL | STROKES | MEANING | UNICODE |
|---|---|---|---|---|
| 1754 | 耳 | 14 | to hear, to listen, to ask | 805E |

### ONYOMI
ブン、モン
*bun, mon*

### KUNYOMI
き(く)
*ki(ku)*

### VOCABULARY

| | | | | |
|---|---|---|---|---|
| 聞く (き) | to hear; to listen | | 新聞 (しんぶん) | newspaper |
| 聞き (き) | hearing | | 見聞 (けんぶん) | information |
| 聞ゆる (きこ) | famous; celebrated | | 聴聞 (ちょうもん) | listening; hearing |

## STROKE ORDER — How this Kanji is drawn

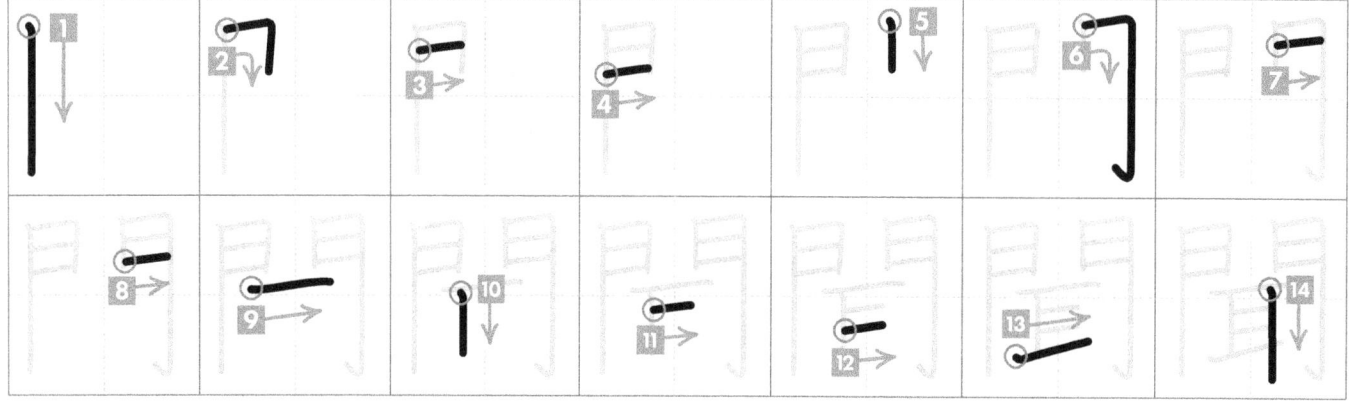

## PRACTICE — Trace and practice this Kanji below

STYLES 聞 聞 聞 聞 聞 聞 聞 聞

| KANJI # | RADICAL | STROKES | MEANING | UNICODE |
|---|---|---|---|---|
| 1582 | 食 | 9 | eat, food | 98DF |

**ONYOMI**
ショク、ジキ
*shoku, jiki*

**KUNYOMI**
く(う)、た(べる)、は(む)
*k(u), ta(beru), ha(mu)*

**VOCABULARY**

| | |
|---|---|
| 食事 (しょくじ) | meal |
| 食品 (しょくひん) | food; food products |
| 食堂 (しょくどう) | dining room |
| 夕食 (ゆうしょく) | evening meal |
| 昼食 (ちゅうしょく) | midday meal |
| 朝食 (ちょうしょく) | breakfast |

**STROKE ORDER** — How this Kanji is drawn

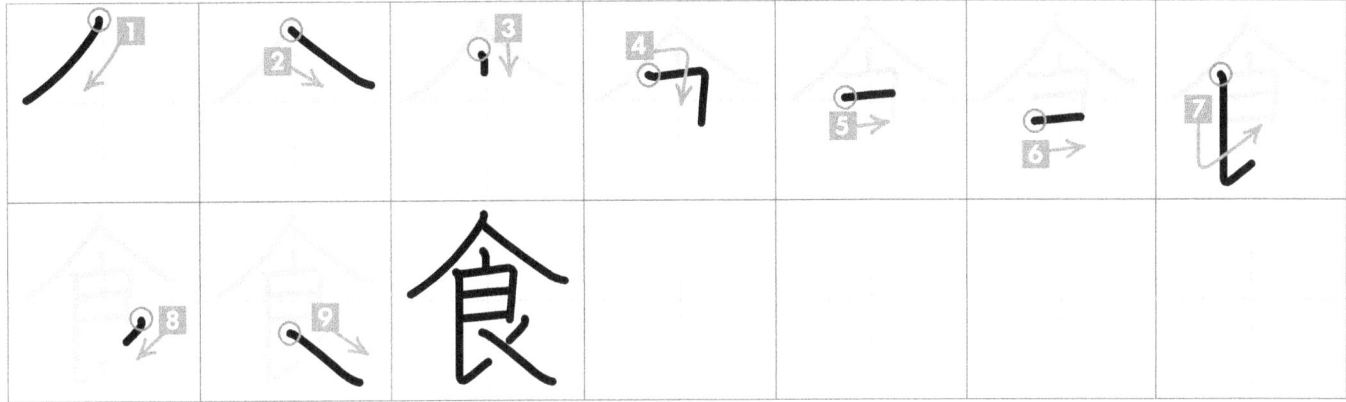

**PRACTICE** — Trace and practice this Kanji below

**STYLES** 食 食 食 食 食 食 食 食

| KANJI # | RADICAL | STROKES | MEANING | | UNICODE |
|---|---|---|---|---|---|
| 0304 | 車 | 7 | car, wheel | | 8ECA |

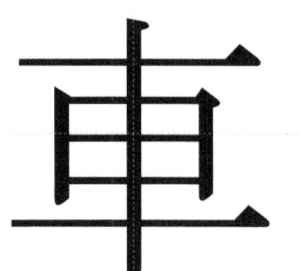

**ONYOMI**
シャ
*sha*

**KUNYOMI**
くるま
*kuruma*

**VOCABULARY**

| | | | |
|---|---|---|---|
| 車輪 (しゃりん) | (car) wheel | 電車 (でんしゃ) | train; electric train |
| 車庫 (しゃこ) | garage; carport | 自動車 (じどうしゃ) | automobile |
| 車内 (しゃない) | inside a train, car, etc | 駐車 (ちゅうしゃ) | parking |

**STROKE ORDER** — How this Kanji is drawn

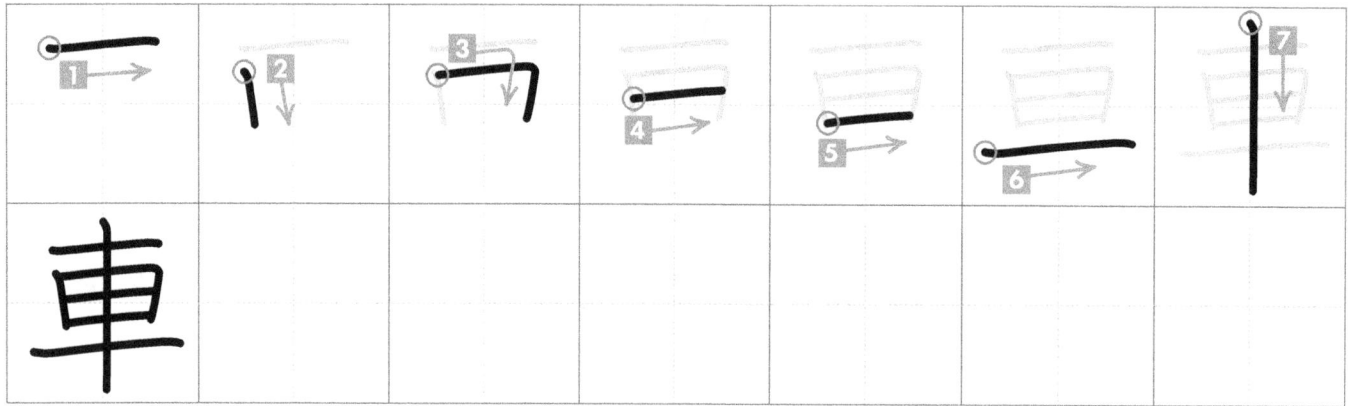

**PRACTICE** — Trace and practice this Kanji below

**STYLES** 車 車 車 車 車 車 車

| KANJI # | RADICAL | STROKES | MEANING | UNICODE |
|---|---|---|---|---|
| 1087 | 人 | 7 | what | 4F55 |

何

**ONYOMI**
カ
*ka*

**KUNYOMI**
なに、なん
*nani, nan*

**VOCABULARY**

| | | | |
|---|---|---|---|
| 何時 (いつ) | when; how soon | 如何 (どう) | how; in what way |
| 何処 (どこ) | where; what place | 幾何 (きか) | geometry |
| 何か (なに) | something | 何々 (なになに) | what is the matter |

## STROKE ORDER
*How this Kanji is drawn*

## PRACTICE
*Trace and practice this Kanji below*

## STYLES
何 何 何 何 何 何 何

91

| KANJI # | RADICAL | STROKES | MEANING | UNICODE |
|---|---|---|---|---|
| 1740 | 十 | 9 | south | 5357 |

南

**ONYOMI**
ナン、ナ
*nan, na*

**KUNYOMI**
みなみ
*minami*

**VOCABULARY**

| | | | |
|---|---|---|---|
| 南北 (なんぼく) | north and south | 東南 (とうなん) | south-east |
| 南西 (なんせい) | southwest | 西南 (せいなん) | south-west |
| 南東 (なんとう) | southeast | 真南 (まみなみ) | due south |

## STROKE ORDER
*How this Kanji is drawn*

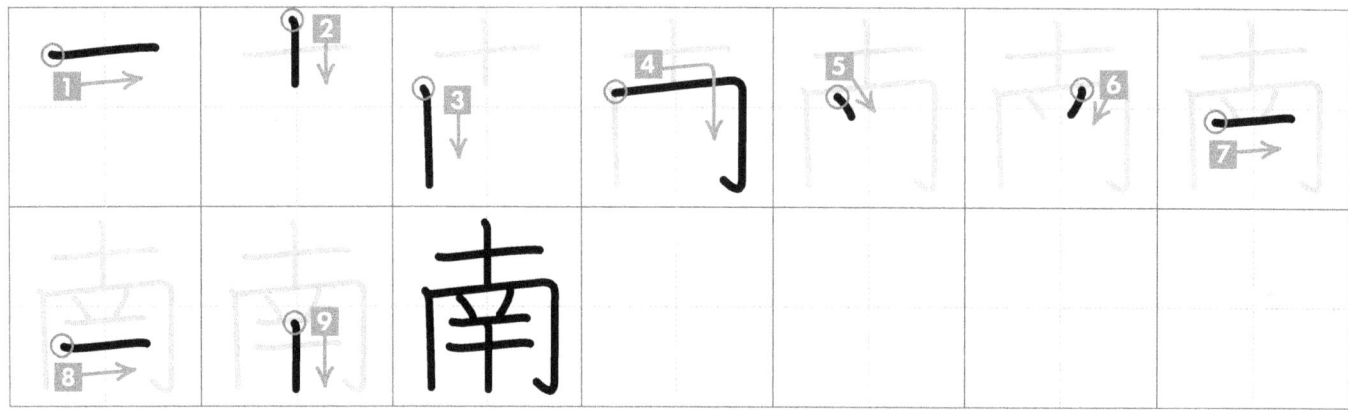

## PRACTICE
*Trace and practice this Kanji below*

STYLES  南 南 南 南 南 南 南

| KANJI # | RADICAL | STROKES | MEANING | UNICODE |
|---|---|---|---|---|
| 0068 | 一 | 3 | ten thousand, 10,000 | 4E07 |

万

**ONYOMI**

マン、バン

*man, ban*

**VOCABULARY**

| | | | |
|---|---|---|---|
| 万一 (まんいち) | emergency | 百万 (ひゃくまん) | one million |
| 万人 (ばんにん) | all people; everybody | 十万 (じゅうまん) | hundred thousand |
| 万能 (ばんのう) | all-purpose; utility | 億万 (おくまん) | millions and millions |

**STROKE ORDER** — How this Kanji is drawn

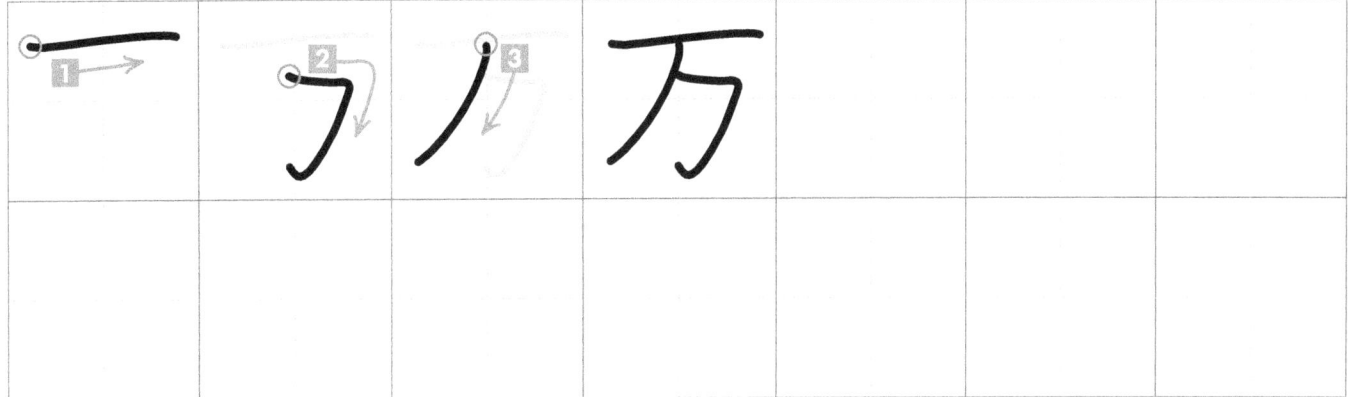

**PRACTICE** — Trace and practice this Kanji below

**STYLES** 万 万 万 万 万 万 万 万

| KANJI # | RADICAL | STROKES | MEANING | UNICODE |
|---|---|---|---|---|
| 0497 | 母 | 6 | **every** | 6BCE |

### ONYOMI
マイ
*mai*

### KUNYOMI
ごと(に)
*goto(ni)*

### VOCABULARY

| | | | | |
|---|---|---|---|---|
| 毎日 (まいにち) | every day | | 丸毎 (まるごと) | in its entirety |
| 毎月 (まいつき) | every month | | 人毎 (ひとごと) | with each person |
| 毎年 (まいとし) | every year | | 毎回 (まいかい) | every time |

## STROKE ORDER
*How this Kanji is drawn*

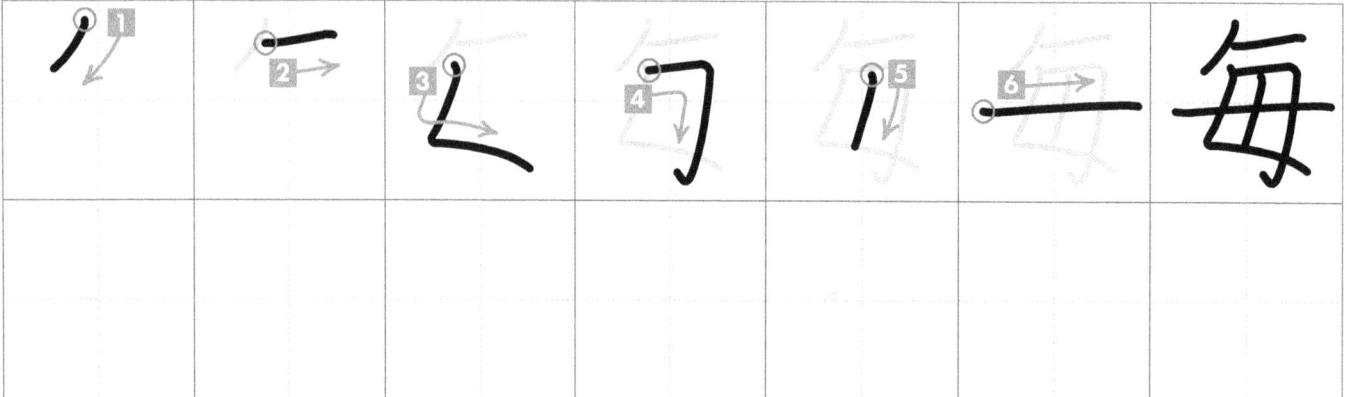

## PRACTICE
*Trace and practice this Kanji below*

STYLES 毎 毎 毎 毎 毎 毎 毎 毎

| KANJI # | RADICAL | STROKES | MEANING | UNICODE |
|---|---|---|---|---|
| 0037 | 白 | 5 | white | 767D |

**ONYOMI**

ハク、ビャク
*haku, byaku*

**KUNYOMI**

しろ(い)
*shiro(i)*

**VOCABULARY**

| | | | |
|---|---|---|---|
| 白書 (はくしょ) | white paper | 告白 (こくはく) | confession |
| 白銀 (しろがね) | silver (ag) | 真っ白 (まっしろ) | pure white; blank |
| 白髪 (しらが) | white hair; gray hair | 空白 (くうはく) | blank space |

## STROKE ORDER

*How this Kanji is drawn*

## PRACTICE

*Trace and practice this Kanji below*

## STYLES

白 白 白 白 白 白 白 白

| KANJI # | RADICAL | STROKES | MEANING | UNICODE |
|---|---|---|---|---|
| 0457 | 大 | 4 | **heavens, sky, imperial** | 5929 |

**ONYOMI**
テン
*ten*

**KUNYOMI**
あまつ, あめ, てん
*amatsu, ame, ama*

**VOCABULARY**

天気 (てんき) — weather
天国 (てんごく) — paradise; heaven
天井 (てんじょう) — ceiling; ceiling price

雨天 (うてん) — rainy weather
楽天 (らくてん) — optimism
炎天 (えんてん) — blazing heat

**STROKE ORDER** — How this Kanji is drawn

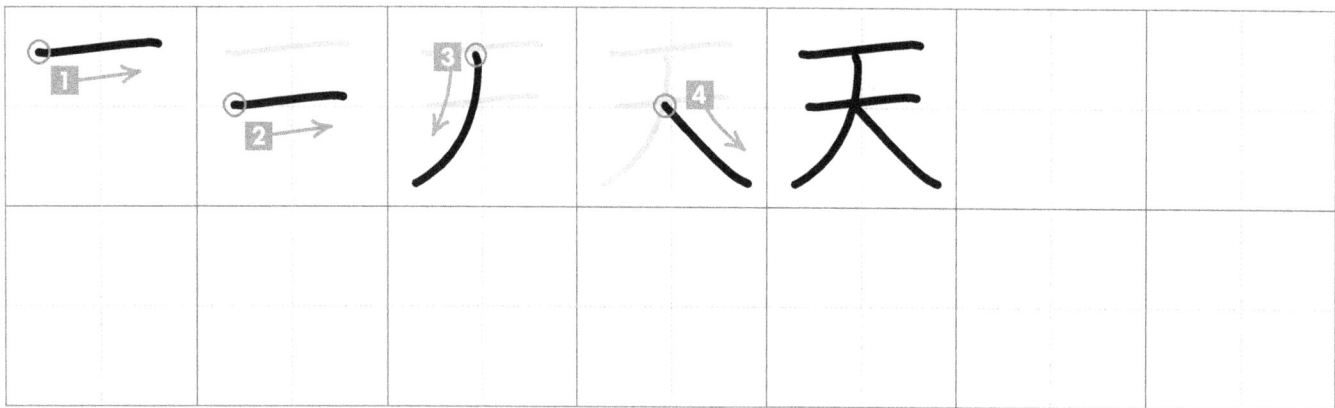

**PRACTICE** — Trace and practice this Kanji below

**STYLES**

| KANJI # | RADICAL | STROKES | MEANING | | UNICODE |
|---|---|---|---|---|---|
| 0105 | 母 | 5 | mother | | 6BCD |

**ONYOMI**
ボ
*bo*

**KUNYOMI**
はは、かあ
*haha, kaa*

**VOCABULARY**

| | | | |
|---|---|---|---|
| 母校 (ぼこう) | alma mater | 祖母 (そぼ) | grandmother |
| 母子 (ぼし) | mother and child | 父母 (ふぼ) | father and mother |
| 母国 (ぼこく) | one's homeland | 分母 (ぶんぼ) | denominator |

**STROKE ORDER** — How this Kanji is drawn

**PRACTICE** — Trace and practice this Kanji below

**STYLES**

97

| KANJI # | RADICAL | STROKES | MEANING | | UNICODE |
|---------|---------|---------|---------|---|---------|
| 0173 | 火 | 4 | fire | | 706B |

## 火

**ONYOMI**

カ
*ka*

**KUNYOMI**

ひ、-び、ほ-
*hi, bi, ho*

**VOCABULARY**

| 火山 (かざん) | volcano | 花火 (はなび) | fireworks |
| 火曜 (かよう) | Tuesday | 灯火 (あかり) | light; glow |
| 火星 (かせい) | Mars (planet) | 噴火 (ふんか) | eruption |

## STROKE ORDER
*How this Kanji is drawn*

## PRACTICE
*Trace and practice this Kanji below*

## STYLES

| KANJI # | RADICAL | STROKES | MEANING | UNICODE |
|---------|---------|---------|---------|---------|
| 0082 | 口 | 5 | right | 53F3 |

**ONYOMI**
ウ、ユウ
*u, yuu*

**KUNYOMI**
みぎ
*migi*

**VOCABULARY**

| | | | |
|---|---|---|---|
| 右手 (みぎて) | right hand | 左右 (さゆう) | left and right |
| 右翼 (うよく) | right-wing (politics) | 上右 (うえみぎ) | upper right |
| 右舷 (うげん) | starboard | 下右 (したみぎ) | lower right |

## STROKE ORDER
*How this Kanji is drawn*

## PRACTICE
*Trace and practice this Kanji below*

## STYLES

右 右 右 右 右 右 右 右

99

| KANJI # | RADICAL | STROKES | MEANING | UNICODE |
|---|---|---|---|---|
| 0372 | 言 | 14 | to read | 8AAD |

**ONYOMI**
ドク、トク、トウ
*doku, toku, tou*

**KUNYOMI**
よ(む)
*yo(mu)*

**VOCABULARY**

| | | | | |
|---|---|---|---|---|
| 読書 (どくしょ) | reading | | 一読 (いちどく) | perusal |
| 読者 (どくしゃ) | reader | | 解読 (かいどく) | deciphering |
| 読本 (とくほん) | reading-book | | 下読 (したよみ) | rehearsal (of play) |

## STROKE ORDER
*How this Kanji is drawn*

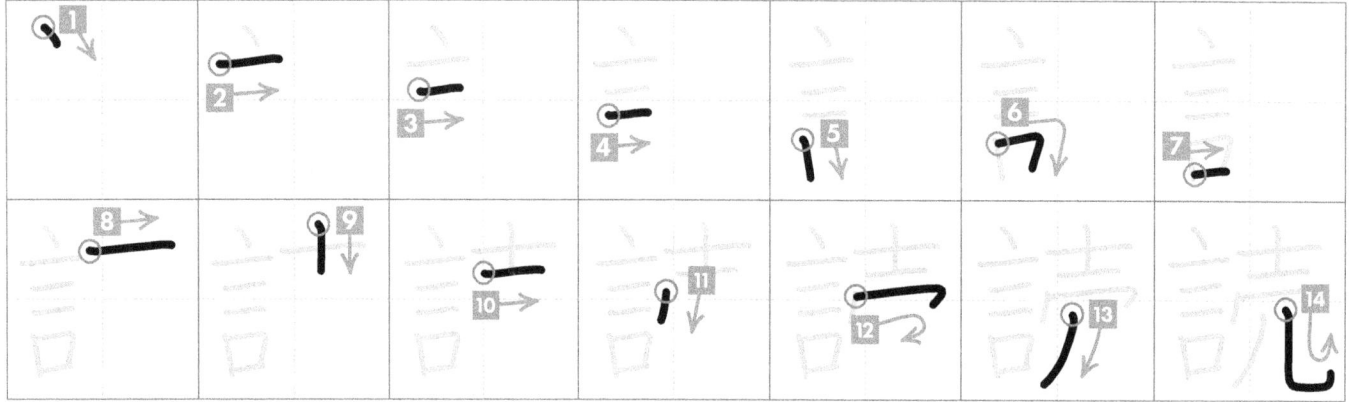

## PRACTICE
*Trace and practice this Kanji below*

STYLES 読 **読** 読 読 **読** 読 読 読

100

| KANJI # | RADICAL | STROKES | MEANING | UNICODE |
|---------|---------|---------|---------|---------|
| 0760 | 又 | 4 | friend | 53CB |

**ONYOMI**
ユウ
*yuu*

**KUNYOMI**
とも
*tomo*

**VOCABULARY**

| | | | |
|---|---|---|---|
| 友好 (ゆうこう) | friendship | 親友 (しんゆう) | close friend |
| 友愛 (ゆうあい) | fraternity | 学友 (がくゆう) | school friend |
| 友邦 (ゆうほう) | friendly nation | 校友 (こうゆう) | schoolmate |

## STROKE ORDER
*How this Kanji is drawn*

## PRACTICE
*Trace and practice this Kanji below*

## STYLES

| KANJI # | RADICAL | STROKES | MEANING | | UNICODE |
|---|---|---|---|---|---|
| 0081 | 工 | 5 | left | | 5DE6 |

左

**ONYOMI**
サ、シャ
*sa, sha*

**KUNYOMI**
ひだり
*hidari*

**VOCABULARY**

左右 (さゆう) — left and right
左手 (ひだりて) — left hand
左腕 (さわん) — left arm

上左 (うえひだり) — upper left
下左 (したひだり) — lower left
極左 (きょくさ) — extreme left

## STROKE ORDER
*How this Kanji is drawn*

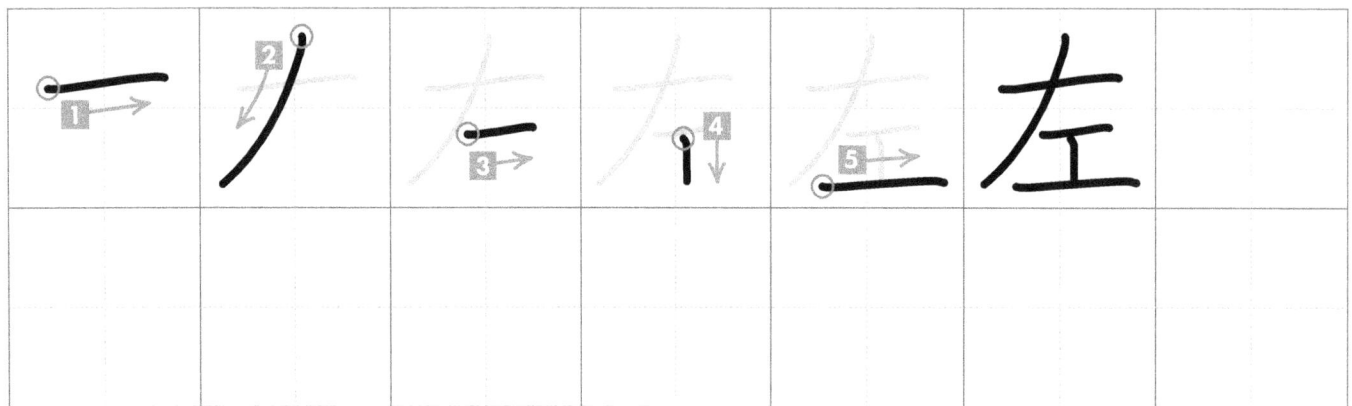

## PRACTICE
*Trace and practice this Kanji below*

STYLES 左 左 左 左 左 左 左 左

| KANJI # | RADICAL | STROKES | MEANING | UNICODE |
|---|---|---|---|---|
| 1038 | 人 | 6 | rest, day off, retire, sleep | 4F11 |

**ONYOMI**
キュウ
*kyuu*

**KUNYOMI**
やす(む)
*yasu(mu)*

**VOCABULARY**

| | | | |
|---|---|---|---|
| 休む (やす) | to be absent | 連休 (れんきゅう) | consecutive holidays |
| 休日 (きゅうじつ) | holiday; day off | 週休 (しゅうきゅう) | weekly holiday |
| 休止 (きゅうし) | pause; cessation | 運休 (うんきゅう) | service suspended |

## STROKE ORDER — How this Kanji is drawn

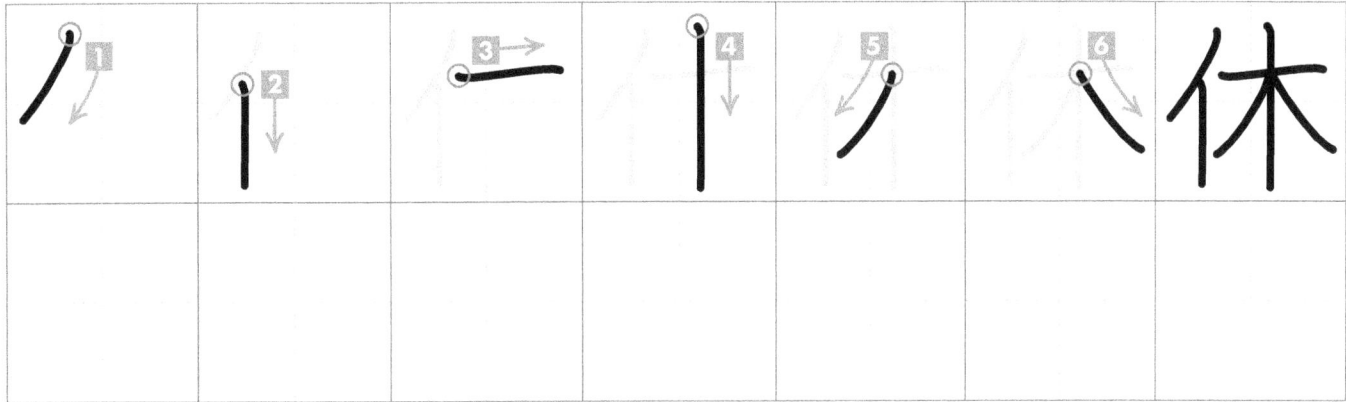

## PRACTICE — Trace and practice this Kanji below

**STYLES**  休 休 休 休 休 休 休 休

| KANJI # | RADICAL | STROKES | MEANING | UNICODE |
|---|---|---|---|---|
| 1366 | 父 | 4 | father | 7236 |

**ONYOMI**

フ
*fu*

**KUNYOMI**

ちち、とう
*chichi, tou*

**VOCABULARY**

父母 (ふぼ) — father and mother
父子 (ふし) — father and child
父兄 (ふけい) — guardians

祖父 (そふ) — grandfather
伯父 (おじ) — uncle
親父 (おやじ) — one's father

## STROKE ORDER
How this Kanji is drawn

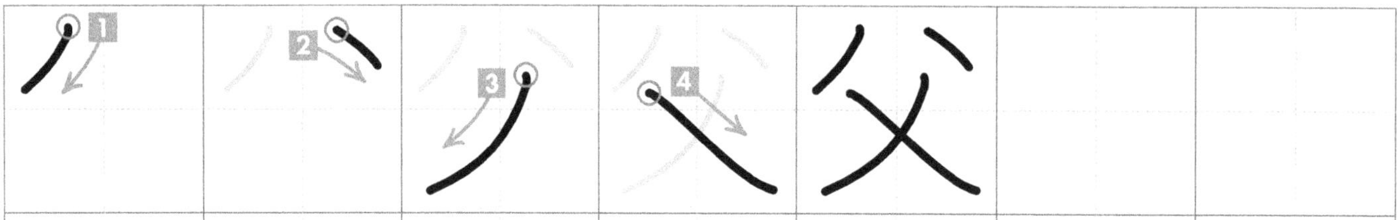

## PRACTICE
Trace and practice this Kanji below

**STYLES**

| KANJI # | RADICAL | STROKES | MEANING | UNICODE |
|---|---|---|---|---|
| 0451 | 雨 | 8 | rain | 96E8 |

**ONYOMI**

ウ
*u*

**KUNYOMI**

あめ、あま
*ame, ama*

**VOCABULARY**

| | | | |
|---|---|---|---|
| 雨天 (うてん) | rainy weather | 梅雨 (つゆ) | rainy season |
| 雨水 (うすい) | rain water | 大雨 (おおあめ) | heavy rain |
| 雨量 (うりょう) | rainfall | 時雨 (しぐれ) | drizzle |

## STROKE ORDER — How this Kanji is drawn

## PRACTICE — Trace and practice this Kanji below

## STYLES

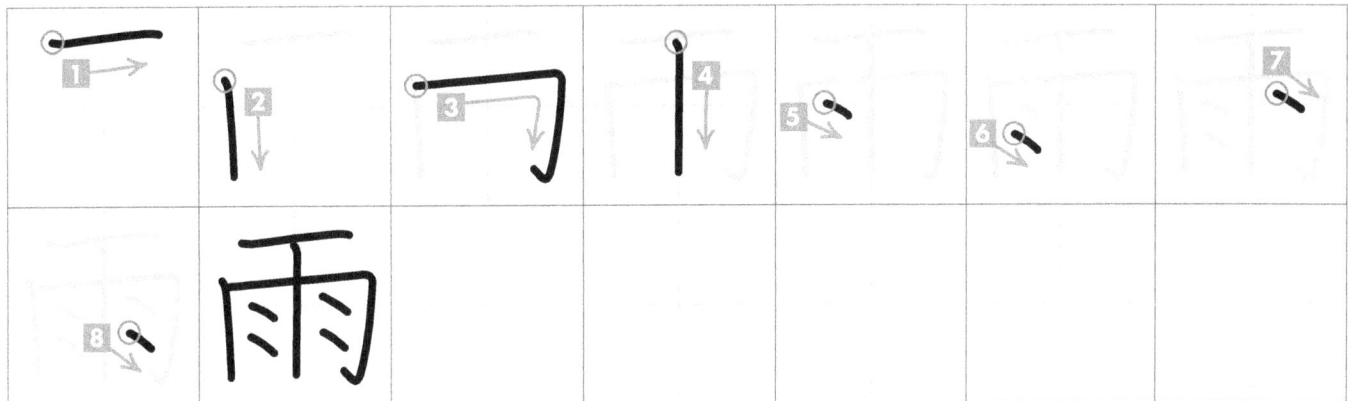

105

## Part 4

# GENKOUYOUSHI
## GRID PAPER FOR FURTHER PRACTICE

## Part 5

# FLASH CARDS
## PHOTOCOPY OR CUT OUT & KEEP

| 日 | 一 | 国 |
|---|---|---|
| 人 | 年 | 大 |
| 本 | 二 | 十 |
| 甲 | 长 | 中 |

| MEANING | day, sun, Japan, counter for days | RADICAL | 日 |
|---|---|---|---|
| MEANING | one | RADICAL | 一 |
| MEANING | country | RADICAL | 口 |

| MEANING | person | RADICAL | 人 |
|---|---|---|---|
| MEANING | year, counter for years | RADICAL | 千 |
| MEANING | large, big | RADICAL | 大 |

| MEANING | book present, true, counter for long cylinders | RADICAL | 木 |
|---|---|---|---|
| MEANING | two, 2 | RADICAL | 二 |
| MEANING | ten, 10 | RADICAL | 十 |

| MEANING | exit, leave, go out | RADICAL | 凵 |
|---|---|---|---|
| MEANING | long, leader, superior, senior | RADICAL | 長 |
| MEANING | in, inside, middle, mean, center | RADICAL | 丨 |

| 行 | 時 | 三 |
| --- | --- | --- |
| 分 | 月 | 見 |
| 生 | 前 | 後 |
| 上 | 間 | 五 |

| MEANING | RADICAL |
|---|---|
| going, journey, carry out, line, row 行 | 行 |

| MEANING | RADICAL |
|---|---|
| time, hour 日 | 日 |

| MEANING | RADICAL |
|---|---|
| part, minute of time, understand 刀 | 刀 |

| MEANING | RADICAL |
|---|---|
| life, genuine, birth 生 | 生 |

| MEANING | RADICAL |
|---|---|
| above, up 一 | 一 |

| MEANING | RADICAL |
|---|---|
| three, 3 一 | 一 |

| MEANING | RADICAL |
|---|---|
| month, moon 月 | 月 |

| MEANING | RADICAL |
|---|---|
| see, hopes, chances, idea, opinion, look at 見 | 見 |

| MEANING | RADICAL |
|---|---|
| in front, before 刀 | 刀 |

| MEANING | RADICAL |
|---|---|
| behind, back, later 彳 | 彳 |

| MEANING | RADICAL |
|---|---|
| interval, space 門 | 門 |

| MEANING | RADICAL |
|---|---|
| five, 5 二 | 二 |

| MEANING | MEANING | MEANING |
|---|---|---|
| now, the present | enter, insert | eight, 8 |
| 今 | 入 | 八 |
| RADICAL 人 | RADICAL 入 | RADICAL 八 |

| MEANING | MEANING | MEANING |
|---|---|---|
| four, 4 | nine, 9 | circle, yen (Japanese monetary unit), round |
| 四 | 九 | 円 |
| RADICAL 囗 | RADICAL 乙 | RADICAL 冂 |

| MEANING | MEANING | MEANING |
|---|---|---|
| east | gold | tall, high, expensive |
| 東 | 金 | 高 |
| RADICAL 木 | RADICAL 金 | RADICAL 高 |

| MEANING | MEANING | MEANING |
|---|---|---|
| | | study, learning, science |
| | 外 | 学 |
| | outside | |
| | RADICAL 夕 | RADICAL 子 |

| MEANING |
|---|
| child |
| 子 |
| RADICAL 子 |

| 来 | 下 | 六 |
| --- | --- | --- |
| 七 | 小 | 気 |
| 女 | 語 | 口 |
| 百 | 午 | 北 |

| MEANING | RADICAL |
|---|---|
| come, due, next, cause, become | 木 |

| MEANING | RADICAL |
|---|---|
| seven, 7 | 一 |

| MEANING | RADICAL |
|---|---|
| woman, female | 女 |

| MEANING | RADICAL |
|---|---|
| hundred | 白 |

| MEANING | RADICAL |
|---|---|
| below, down, descend, give, low, inferior | 口 |

| MEANING | RADICAL |
|---|---|
| little, small | 小 |

| MEANING | RADICAL |
|---|---|
| tale, talk | 言 |

| MEANING | RADICAL |
|---|---|
| noon, sign of the horse | 十 |

| MEANING | RADICAL |
|---|---|
| six, 6 | 八 |

| MEANING | RADICAL |
|---|---|
| spirit, mind, air, atmosphere, mood | 气 |

| MEANING | RADICAL |
|---|---|
| moutain | 山 |

| MEANING | RADICAL |
|---|---|
| north | 匕 |

| 名 | 先 | 書 |
| --- | --- | --- |
| 水 | 千 | 川 |
| 西 | 男 | 半 |
| 語 | 校 | 電 |

| 鼠 | 长 | 土 |
| --- | --- | --- |
| 何 | 田 | 食 |
| 角 | 力 | 西 |
| 申 | 天 | 日 |

| MEANING | RADICAL |
|---|---|
| soil, earth, ground | 土 |

| MEANING | RADICAL |
|---|---|
| tree, wood | 木 |

| MEANING | RADICAL |
|---|---|
| to hear, to listen, to ask | 耳 |

| MEANING | RADICAL |
|---|---|
| what | 人 |

| MEANING | RADICAL |
|---|---|
| car, wheel | 車 |

| MEANING | RADICAL |
|---|---|
| eat, food | 食 |

| MEANING | RADICAL |
|---|---|
| every | 毋 |

| MEANING | RADICAL |
|---|---|
| ten thousand, 10,000 | 一 |

| MEANING | RADICAL |
|---|---|
| south | 十 |

| MEANING | RADICAL |
|---|---|
| mother | 毋 |

| MEANING | RADICAL |
|---|---|
| heavens, sky, imperial | 大 |

| MEANING | RADICAL |
|---|---|
| white | 白 |

| 読 | 右 | 火 |
| --- | --- | --- |
| 休 | 左 | 友 |
|  | 用 | 父 |

| MEANING | to read | RADICAL | 言 |
| --- | --- | --- | --- |
| MEANING | rest, day off, retire, sleep | RADICAL | 人 |

| MEANING | right | RADICAL | 口 |
| --- | --- | --- | --- |
| MEANING | left | RADICAL | 工 |

| MEANING | fire | RADICAL | 火 |
| --- | --- | --- | --- |
| MEANING | rain | RADICAL | 雨 |

| MEANING | friend | RADICAL | 又 |
| --- | --- | --- | --- |
| MEANING | father | RADICAL | 父 |

# ありがとう
arigatou

# Thank you!

**Thank you for choosing our book!**

You are now well on your way to learning how to read, write and speak Japanese, and we hope that you enjoyed our Kanji workbook.

If you enjoyed learning with us, we would very much like to hear about your progress in a review!

We are always eager to learn if there is anything we can do to make our books better for future students. We are committed to making the best language learning content available so please do get in touch with us via email if you had a problem with any of the content in this book:

**hello@polyscholar.com**

POLYSCHOLAR

www.polyscholar.com

© Copyright 2020 George Tanaka - **All rights reserved.**

Legal Notice: This book is copyright protected. This book is only for personal use. The content contained within this book may not be reproduced, duplicated or transmitted without direct written permission from the author or the publisher. You cannot amend, distribute, sell, use, quote or paraphrase any part of the content within this book, without the consent of the author or publisher.

www.ingramcontent.com/pod-product-compliance
Lightning Source LLC
Chambersburg PA
CBHW060416010526
44107CB00006B/709